# CANNABIS
## COCKTAILS,
## MOCKTAILS & TONICS

········· THE ART OF ·········

## SPIRITED DRINKS &
## BUZZ-WORTHY LIBATIONS

### WARREN
### BOBROW

FAIR WINDS

Inspiring | Educating | Creating | Entertaining

Brimming with creative inspiration, how-to projects, and useful information to enrich your everyday life, Quarto Knows is a favorite destination for those pursuing their interests and passions. Visit our site and dig deeper with our books into your area of interest: Quarto Creates, Quarto Cooks, Quarto Homes, Quarto Lives, Quarto Drives, Quarto Explores, Quarto Gifts, or Quarto Kids.

© 2016 Quarto Publishing Group USA Inc.
Text © 2016 Warren Bobrow

First published in 2016 by Fair Winds Press,
an imprint of The Quarto Group,
100 Cummings Center, Suite 265-D,
Beverly, MA 01915, USA.
T (978) 282-9590 F (978) 283-2742
www.QuartoKnows.com

Fair Winds Press titles are also available at discount for retail, wholesale, promotional, and bulk purchase. For details, contact the Special Sales Manager by email at specialsales@quarto.com or by mail at The Quarto Group, Attn: Special Sales Manager, 401 Second Avenue North, Suite 310, Minneapolis, MN 55401, USA.

20 19 18 17          4 5

ISBN: 978-1-59233-734-7

Digital edition published in 2016
eISBN: 978-1-63159-177-8

Library of Congress Cataloging-in-Publication Data Available

Design: Sussner Design Company
Page Layout: Kathie Alexander
Photography: Glenn Scott Photography
Food Styling: Natasha Taylor, natasha-taylor-stilllife.squarespace.com

Printed in China

MIX
Paper from responsible sources
FSC
www.fsc.org   FSC® C104723

The distilled spirit producers featured in this book do not condone/support/promote the simultaneous consumption of alcohol and marijuana, nor were they involved in the production of this book. The distilled spirit producers featured in this book do not condone/support/promote the purchase, sale, or use of federally controlled substances.

*To my father,*
ROBERT BOBROW,
*who taught me to stand on
my own two feet and succeed
at what made me happy.*

# FOREWORD

## ALCOHOL + CANNABIS: Why It Matters

**M**arijuana is enjoying increased social acceptance and even legalization in some states. At first glance one might conclude that the legalization of marijuana isn't that different from the end of the prohibition against alcohol. An intoxicant was illegal, now it isn't.

Yes, that's true—but with a big difference. Both alcohol and marijuana alter one's consciousness, but science is showing that cannabis makes us feel good and it may have properties that heal us as well. Cannabis is proving helpful in alleviating the side effects of cancer, particularly pain and nausea. It is showing promise in alleviating the anxiety and depression of PTSD, and alleviating some symptoms of Crohn's disease.

Modern science is uncovering the science behind medical marijuana, and with these discoveries our relationship to this once forbidden plant is quickly evolving. No longer shunned and hidden, the wave of legalization sweeping the world is opening doors for so many of us.

I see three chapters in this amazing story: decriminalization (including medical marijuana), legalization (even with conditions and fine print), and finally normalization. Normalization occurs when cannabis takes its rightful place in modern life. Not shunned or ostracized, but on the shelf next to your other consumer goods.

While cooking with cannabis is a well-established practice, using cannabis in cocktails is relatively new. Ethanol is an excellent solvent for all that's good in cannabis. Whether your objective is to capture the cannabinoids, like THC and CBD, or to impart a one-of-a-kind flavor by stripping terpenes and flavonoids, alcohol is your best alternative. It's inexpensive, nontoxic compared to other industrial solvents, and let's face it, you need alcohol to make cocktails anyway!

There is more to cannabis cocktails than mixing two intoxicants together and getting buzzed. If one applies solid science to mixing cannabis into cocktails not only are unique and exotic flavors at the tip of your tongue—but one can use precise methods and techniques to elevate a mere beverage to an herbal concoction.

It's all well and good to say, "Use cannabis in your drinks." But the how is more important than the what. No one is advocating tossing a joint in the blender and making a libation. Not only would you fail to get high or impart a desirable flavor, you're doing little more than throwing money away while displaying your ignorance about the chemistry of cannabis.

We all need a guide, a docent, someone to lead the way. This person needs to bridge the worlds of booze and bud, potables and pot. And this person needs to understand the chemistry behind what they're doing. One such person can lead all of us to healthier cocktails that combine the best of both worlds. Formulations that bring out the wonderful properties of cannabis. Recipes we can all make at home with the bar and kitchen tools we already have.

With three books to his credit, Warren Bobrow has already proven to us all he knows what he's doing. With this book, he's sharing some of the science behind cannabis cocktails with style and finesse.

JERRY WHITING
*LeBlanc CNE / Seattle*

# CONTENTS

# INTRODUCTION

Cannabis has been used as herbal medicine for thousands of years at the very least, in ancient Chinese and Egyptian cultures, among others. Eventually it made its way around the world, including Europe and the United States, where it became illegal in the 1930s. These days, a number of states have either decriminalized cannabis or permit its use for medical purposes—it's been said to help with pain relief, muscle spasms, and chemotherapy-induced nausea and vomiting, for instance.

You probably know that the traditional way to ingest cannabis is to smoke it. But if you don't enjoy smoking, or if you're worried about the health risks associated with smoking, it's hard to know what else to do with cannabis— except add it to baked goods, of course. And let's face it: you can only eat so many pot brownies.

There is an alternative, though. Craft cocktails are a new, and increasingly popular, way to consume cannabis. And that's where this book comes in. It'll teach you everything you need to know about using cannabis in both cocktails and mocktails—and how to do it safely and effectively.

If the combination of craft cocktails and cannabis sounds unusual to you, it might surprise you to learn that small amounts of cannabis can actually complement some spirits. After all, cocktail bitters—every bartender's best friend—originated as herbal medicines in early apothecaries. Bitters contained (and still contain) medicinal botanicals that were intended to ease maladies of all sorts. From that perspective, then, it is a pretty logical step to add cannabis to *digestifs*, such as amaro, or to gut-friendly, vinegar-based shrubs. And, most importantly, when they're made well, cannabis cocktails taste good.

## Are cannabis cocktails right for me?

To help you decide whether the recipes in this book are right for you, let's talk about what *Cannabis Cocktails* is *not*. If you're looking for a get-stoned-quick cookbook, look elsewhere: you won't learn how to do that here. Instead, you'll learn how to craft refreshing, well-balanced cocktails and mocktails in which cannabis is simply another ingredient.

---

**MODERATION IS KEY.** WHEN YOU'RE CONSUMING CANNABIS—AND ESPECIALLY WHEN YOU'RE PAIRING IT WITH ALCOHOL—IT'S VITAL TO REMEMBER THAT LESS IS MORE. SO WHATEVER YOU DO, DON'T OVERDO IT. START WITH DOSES OF 10 MG OF CANNABIS AND MOVE FORWARD FROM THERE, IF AND WHEN YOU'RE READY. AND, WHEN YOU'RE MAKING DRINKS THAT CONTAIN CANNABIS, ALWAYS USE LESS ALCOHOL THAN YOU WOULD IN A REGULAR COCKTAIL. REMEMBER, THIS ISN'T A HORSE RACE: IT'S ABOUT GAUGING YOUR OWN INDIVIDUAL REACTIONS. FOR MORE ON HOW TO CONSUME CANNABIS AND ALCOHOL SAFELY, SEE PAGE 11.

Still interested? If so, here's how the careful addition of cannabis can help enhance your homemade cocktails. You'll be able to:

**Enjoy new flavors, textures, and scents.** Just like aromatic bitters or flavored simple syrups, cannabis can add flavor and dimension to cocktails. And by flavor, I don't just mean "essence of burnt funk!" From a purely culinary standpoint, the flavors inherent to cannabis can be incredibly intriguing: they might be reminiscent of citrus fruits, tropical fruits, pine needles, or menthol. Combine those flavors with well-chosen cocktail ingredients, such as freshly squeezed fruit juices and liquors, and the results are delicious. As with all food and drink, taste is subjective. You might find that you're drawn to some of the recipes in this book more than others—and that's perfectly fine. But I think you'll agree that these cocktails and mocktails have been crafted to be nuanced and well-balanced, and they aren't laced with that "skunky" taste that's typical to cannabis.

**Get smoke-free pain relief.** If you use cannabis for medical purposes, adding it to your beverages means that you'll be able to consume it without having to smoke it. That's a huge plus: even if smoking doesn't bother you personally, lots of people are put off by the pungent aroma of the burning herb. Besides, you might simply find

that it's more pleasurable to drink your medicinals than it is to inhale them.

**Achieve a precise dosage.** Enjoying a single cocktail is far easier than eating a bunch of pot brownies—and, because you'll be able to achieve an accurate dosage every time, you'll be less likely to hurt yourself by over-ingesting. (With traditional edibles like baked goods, it's hard to determine exactly how much THC or CBD exists in each bite.) It seems that the pain-reducing effects of cannabis are felt more quickly when they're consumed in a beverage, too.

**Make cannabis more tolerable.** You may find that you're better able to tolerate cannabis when you eat or drink it rather than smoke it. That's good to know if you're a medical cannabis user, and need to use it regularly. Of course, each person's reaction to cannabis is different, so you won't know how your body tolerates it best until you try consuming it in different ways. Ultimately, though, you should take the recommendations of the caregiver at your dispensary very seriously. He or she will be familiar with the individual strains of cannabis and their effects, and will be able to advise you—and to suggest a recommended dosage.

Now that you're on board with my philosophy on cannabis use, it's time to start making flavorful, diverse, aroma-driven cocktails and mocktails! But first, here's what to expect in the coming pages. I'll give you a

**CANNABIS ISN'T KID-FRIENDLY.** CANNABIS PRODUCTS SHOULD NEVER BE GIVEN TO CHILDREN UNLESS SPECIFICALLY RECOMMENDED BY A MEDICAL DOCTOR. BE SURE TO KEEP YOUR CANNABIS AND CANNABIS-INFUSED PRODUCTS SAFELY AWAY FROM KIDS.

**PLAY IT SAFE.** RESPONSIBLE CANNABIS USE IS AS IMPORTANT AS RESPONSIBLE ALCOHOL USE. THAT MEANS COMBINING ALCOHOL AND CANNABIS HAS TO BE DONE WITH THE UTMOST CARE. CANNABIS CAN BE A POWERFUL INTOXICANT IF IT'S USED INCORRECTLY (ESPECIALLY IF YOU'RE PAIRING IT WITH ALCOHOL). SO, IT'S ABSOLUTELY ESSENTIAL THAT YOU FOLLOW—NO, MEMORIZE—THESE SAFETY TIPS BEFORE YOU TRY ANY OF THE RECIPES IN THIS BOOK. TATTOO THEM ON YOUR FOREARM, IF YOU MUST.

- **Start with—and consider sticking with—a very small dose.** For instance, placing a single drop of a concentrated cannabis tincture under the tongue and holding it there for 30 seconds can have a very powerful effect. And that's just one drop! Never use more than a couple drops in a cocktail with alcohol—and if you're new to cannabis cocktails, start with even less. As with food, so with cocktails: You can always add more spice if you need to, but you can't take it out once you've added it, so proceed with care. And if you do use too much cannabis extract in your drinks, stay put. Ask for help if you need it, and whatever you do, don't make any plans to drive.

- **Pay attention to your body's unique reactions.** Each person's tolerance for cannabis is different, and can be influenced by factors such as your lifestyle, your psychological or emotional state, and any medications you might be taking. That's why you need to be mindful of your individual reactions to cannabis, particularly when you're combining it with alcohol. Know your personal limits, and don't exceed them: if you start to feel unwell, stop consuming cannabis immediately.

*(continued on p.12)*

- **Both alcohol and cannabis impair decision-making and motor skills.** That's why it's important to consume cannabis cocktails in a safe place—in your home or in the company of someone you trust.

- **Never drive or operate machinery of any kind after enjoying a cannabis cocktail.** You'd never even consider driving when you're enjoying alcoholic cocktails, so it makes sense that you shouldn't drive when you're using cannabis in any form, including cannabis cocktails.

- **Side effects may take a while to wear off.** It's important to be aware that some side effects of consuming cannabis can last for up to 24 hours after ingestion. Always plan your schedule accordingly. Common side effects include dizziness, tiredness, or nausea. If you find that you're having a negative reaction warm chamomile and lavender tea may alleviate any temporary discomfort.

- **Combining heavily-alcoholic drinks with cannabis can be particularly dangerous.** You'll find that most of the drinks in this book are either nonalcoholic or relatively light in alcohol content, about 2 ounces (60 ml) or less. So, don't be tempted to add an extra dose of liquor to your handmade cocktail. Stick to the proportions recommended in the recipes. Overdoing it is never a good idea.

- **Consult your doctor before use.** As with any type of herbal medicine, you should always consult your doctor before you attempt any non–FDA-approved practices.

**FIND THE RIGHT STRAIN.** THE CRAFT COCKTAILS IN THIS BOOK USE CANNABIS EXTRACTS FROM MANY DIFFERENT STRAINS: FEEL FREE TO USE THE ONES THAT WORK BEST FOR YOU. CHECK OUT CHAPTER 2 TO LEARN MORE ABOUT THE DIFFERENT STRAINS OF CANNABIS.

crash course in apothecary medicine, which is especially relevant because history tells us that the earliest patent medicines contained cannabis. You'll get the rundown on how healing herbals have been used since time immemorial. Then, you'll learn how and why cannabis provides pain relief (not to mention the "high" associated with cannabis use), and why not all leaves are created equal: Different strains of cannabis have different flavor profiles, and produce different results in terms of taste and effect.

In chapter 3, I'll show you how to decarbolize cannabis at home, and how to stock your pantry with the homemade syrups, tonics, infusions, oils, and com-pound butters that you'll use for the recipes in chapters 4 through 9. That's where I'll introduce you to Drinking in New Delhi, a warming, relaxing version of chai tea that's fortified with butter and just the right amount of cannabis tincture. And you'll come face-to-face with the luscious Benny Goodman Fizz, which mixes cannabis-infused

gin with grapefruit bitters, a dash of rose-flavored simple syrup, and a dash of seltzer water: it's ridiculously refreshing, especially on a hot summer's afternoon. And these are just a couple of the seventy-five recipes in this book: they're all my own creations, and they're all brand-new.

As the Cocktail Whisperer, I'm passionate about creating craft cocktails, especially ones that take their inspira-tion from the herbal remedies used by apothecaries and early pharmacists. So, I'm delighted to share these easy-to-make cannabis-infused libations with you. It's my hope that you'll enjoy them as you would any other kind of alcoholic drink: responsibly, considerately, and moderately.

*Cheers!*
WARREN BOBROW

# PART I

# THE BASICS

# 01

## THE HISTORY OF
### *Medical Liquids and Tonics*

Plant-based curatives are as old as oral history. For millennia, folk healers in cultures around the world have used botanicals—including cannabis—to treat a wide variety of conditions, from insomnia to digestive disorders to respiratory illnesses. In this chapter, you'll learn why cannabis has been *persona non grata* in the medical world since the early twentieth century—and why that's starting to change at last. Of course, as our ancestors would have known, mixing cannabis with alcohol has to be done with the utmost care, so here's where you'll learn how to do it as safely and effectively as possible.

America's first licensed pharmacist was New Orleans–based Louis J. Dufilho, Jr., who certainly used cannabis in his herbal preparations. It's likely that he became acquainted with the healing properties of cannabis by interacting with the multitudes of French and Spanish immigrants who were flocking to New Orleans in the nineteenth century. Many of these men and women brought their folk healing methods—and exotic herbs, seeds, and spices—with them on their long and perilous journeys to the New World. The New Orleans Pharmacy Museum, located where Dufilho once plied his trade, displays a wide variety of medicinals (tinctures, tonics, bitters, and elixirs) and cannabis-based healing products, such as "Indian Cigarettes" which consisted of a mixture of cannabis and rare, Louisiana-grown tobacco. After the passage of the Pure Food and Drug Act in 1906, it became illegal to use either alcohol or cannabis in medicinal preparations of any kind.

Like alcohol, cannabis was ousted from early twentieth-century pharmacies—even though its beneficial properties were well known to herbal healers around the world, and had been since time immemorial. But how did cannabis make its way to the United States in the first place? The answer is, most likely, the Spanish, who learned techniques for making hemp into rope from Arab traders. Later, industrial hemp was being shipped to the New World—and along with it, hemp's healing cousin, *Cannabis sativa.*

That's probably how cannabis made its official entrance into the United States. Although some sources suggest that hemp already existed in America well before the Age of Exploration, and that it could have arrived *sub rosa* with other early explorers or migrating birds. In any event, hemp was a valuable commodity by the eighteenth century because it was necessary for making rope. The British Crown required early American settlers to grow hemp for export. And these settlers' servants, many of whom hailed from Africa or the Caribbean, knew how to employ cannabis as part of folk healing. Unfortunately, these healing techniques didn't translate into modern medicine until very recently. To find out why, let's fast-forward to the twentieth century.

At the end of the 1920s—an economically prosperous decade in which literature, art, and jazz music flourished and in which women won the vote—the United States was plunged into the Great Depression. Prohibition, which banned the sale and consumption of alcohol, was in full swing, so it's no wonder that the 1930s was hardly a good time for the legal (read: public) enjoyment of cannabis. Then, after the 1937 Marihuana Tax Act (yes, that's how it was spelled back in the day!), it became illegal to use or possess cannabis, even for medical use. Mass hysteria in the media about the evils of drug addiction equated the use of cannabis with alcohol. And, even though Prohibition ended in 1933, cannabis remained illegal under federal law for decades, although individual states began to decriminalize it or approve it for medical use as early as 1973.

In some ancient cultures, cannabis was thought to promote mental clarity, aid in meditation, and help users achieve spiritual connectivity, but unfortunately, racist twentieth-century lawmakers used it as a tool to discriminate against nonwhites, especially African-Americans. During Prohibition, politicians and the media slammed cannabis as "a drug used by criminals—black and Hispanics alike." The truth, though, was that this was a shameless attempt at social manipulation intended to marginalize or subordinate certain ethnic groups who used cannabis as part of their cultures. (Rastafarians, for example, use it in some religious ceremonies.) And that meant that the beneficial uses of cannabis were conveniently forgotten.

Then, in 1970, the Marihuana Tax Act was repealed and replaced with the Controlled Substances Act. Under it, cannabis was still classified as a Schedule I intoxicant with no medicinal value—alongside highly toxic and addictive drugs including synthetic opiates, morphine, heroin, cocaine, and methamphetamines—despite its

lengthy history in healing practices. Even today, the federal government continues to consider cannabis as a Schedule I intoxicant with no medicinal value.

Nonetheless, cannabis is making a comeback. It's slowly regaining its reputation as a valuable healing herb, and it has been legalized for medical use in some states. These days, cannabis is available in many different formats: chewable, smokable, edible—and even drinkable. And it can be a blessing for some people with serious medical conditions. Some doctors have prescribed it to ease chronic pain, minimize seizures, and to boost appetite (especially in folks who are suffering from the side effects of intense chemotherapy or other synthetic drugs). Some cannabidiol (CBD)-rich cannabis strains may be of potential benefit when it comes to treating psychological conditions such as schizophrenia, as a 2012 article in the journal *Drug Testing and Analysis* indicates.

Cannabis's renaissance isn't just taking place in the United States. I'm not planning on traveling to North Korea anytime soon, and you probably aren't either, but here's a little-known fact: cannabis use is legal in North Korea, so if you happen to find yourself there, go ahead and enjoy it. And, if you're planning on heading elsewhere, you may find yourself pleasantly surprised: Although many countries around the world still treat cannabis like a hard drug, others are rediscovering the medical benefits that cannabis possesses.

The Netherlands seems to be leading the movement toward the relaxation of laws regarding the possession and use of cannabis. Back in the 1980s, I visited Holland to enjoy the museums, the canals, the diverse cuisine, the beers, and, of course, the "coffee shops." Sure, these "coffee shops" poured decent lattés, cappuccinos, and espressos, but they were—and are—best-known for their special selections of high-quality cannabis, either for smoking or ingestion. Yes, Holland has long been unperturbed by the concept of cannabis use, and the sale of medical marijuana in pharmacies was legalized in the Netherlands in 2003. Doctors routinely prescribe it for their patients, not least because its use is socially accepted within Dutch culture.

In Spain, too, cannabis use is legal—at least within private spaces, such as your own home. (Not that I've ever tried it, but if you were caught smoking a joint on the street in Spain, your accoster would probably just escort you to a tapas bar and share a glass of sherry with you.) There are more than five hundred private cannabis clubs in Spain, and its use is quickly becoming more widely sanctioned.

Italy has decriminalized cannabis and made it legal for medical use, which just goes to show that the wine and liquor industry really has nothing to fear when it comes to the legalization of medical cannabis. In Germany, cannabis possession is illegal, but its consumption is not. It's also refreshing to know that German authorities don't waste their time persecuting people who are truly sick: Medical cannabis is legal when it's obtained with a doctor's note plus permission from the appropriate government board. In France, sale, possession, cultivation, and use of cannabis all remain illegal, but some prescription medicines containing cannabis derivatives have been approved.

Meanwhile, Portugal and Switzerland have decriminalized the use of cannabis, but basic possession is still illegal. (If I were you, I'd avoid antagonizing the local constabulary by smoking a joint in public.) However, if a patient needed to self-medicate with a cannabis cocktail in private, it's pretty unlikely that he or she would be prosecuted.

And restrictions on the use of cannabis haven't only been relaxed in Europe. In South America, Uruguay has completely legalized the use of cannabis in any form, while Peru has legalized possession up to 8 grams, and Jamaica has done the same for up to 2 ounces or 56 grams. More countries may soon follow suit as the medical benefits of cannabis become more firmly established.

This relaxation of restrictions on cannabis, and the resurgence in cannabis research, reflect the growing respect for cannabis in the worldwide medical community. For instance, the well-respected *British Journal of Clinical Pharmacology* published several studies from 2012 to the present on the use of cannabidiol for neurodegenerative disorders, such as Parkinson's disease and Alzheimer's disease. And the good news is you don't need to get high to reap the health benefits of cannabis, either. Certain strains of cannabis have been carefully engineered to minimize levels of THC, the compound in cannabis that produces the buzzed or euphoric sensation you get when you consume it.

Different strains can be useful in treating different conditions, and each produces a different physical effect. For example, certain Sativa strains seem to increase mental focus and alertness, making them perfect for daytime use. Indica strains can promote mental and physical relaxation, so they can be ideal for use in the evening. However, each person's needs—and physical reactions—to cannabis strains are individual and unique. You'll want to follow your caregiver's recommendations when it comes to choosing a cannabis strain and timing your dosage.

From apothecary preparations of yore to synthetically derived drugs containing cannabidiol, cannabis has been an integral part of herbal healing in cultures worldwide for, well, as long as humans have been getting sick. But what are the compounds in cannabis that make it such an effective healing agent—and why does it make you feel "high" in the first place? To answer that question, chapter 2 will give you a short course in cannabis science.

**EXPERT JERRY WHITING'S ADVICE ON SAFELY COMBINING CANNABIS AND ALCOHOL.** I'VE SAID IT BEFORE, BUT I'LL SAY IT AGAIN: MIXING CANNABIS AND ALCOHOL SHOULD ONLY BE DONE CAREFULLY AND RESPONSIBLY. AND THAT'S WHY I ASKED EXPERT JERRY WHITING FOR SOME SAFETY ADVICE ON BLENDING THE TWO.

As the founder of LeBlanc CNE, growers and brokers of medical cannabis and vintage heirloom strains, Jerry certainly knows his stuff. LeBlanc has an extensive collection of CBD-rich strains, including a seed bank as well as live plants. It also sponsors a hemp breeding project, does research into the relationship between cannabis chemistry and genetics, and processes cannabis preparations. Plus, Jerry has a background in acupuncture, massage, and natural healing. He is currently engaged in product development for Seattle-based Green Lion Farms (greenlionfarms.com), a business-to-business consultancy firm and manufacturer of product lines focused on the advanced health benefits and results yielded from the vegetation and cultivation of marijuana. He teaches, lectures, and writes on cannabis, and develops software for the cannabis industry.

"Ethyl alcohol is a safe, efficient solvent when it comes to making cannabis preparations," says Jerry. "It's less toxic than other solvents, and it picks up both cannabinoids like THC and CBD, as well as the aromatic terpenes. Alcohol-based cannabis tinctures are a good way to ingest cannabis—and, as an added bonus, they can help make tasty cocktails.

"Still, mixing cannabis and alcohol should be undertaken with caution. Each person's reaction to a cannabis cocktail is individual: and your body reacts differently when you ingest marijuana instead of smoking it. You may not feel the effects of cannabis for up to an hour after you eat or drink it, and it can also make some people anxious and/or jittery. (There's a remedy for that, though: Sniff freshly ground pepper and drink lemonade made with grated lemon peel. Both are full of terpenes: the former contains caryophyllene, and the latter contains limonene. These compounds react with the cannabinoid receptors in your brain to produce a calming effect.) Always start slowly with small servings, pay attention to your own reactions, and let common sense be your guide."

# O2

## CANNABIS CONNOISSEURSHIP

As a trained chef and an expert mixologist, I think the best part of enjoying a great meal or a craft cocktail is being able to appreciate the quality and balance of its ingredients. So, when it comes to creating cannabis cocktails, it's important to understand the chemistry that's responsible for the herb's physical effects and healing properties—as well as the flavor profiles of individual strains.

In this chapter, you'll get a short science lesson on cannabis: you'll find out why consuming cannabis produces a "high," and why some folks prize it for its medical applications. Then, you'll get a brief rundown on some of the cannabis strains I use to prepare ingredients for my cocktails. As with wine, there are literally thousands of different cannabis varietals, so it isn't possible to cover them all here. Each varietal has its own unique taste and scent (and can produce different physical effects). Each can also be paired with a range of different spirits, juices, bitters, shrubs, and other mixers to create delicious drinks.

# The Chemistry Behind Cannabis Preparations

**E**ven if you've never tried it, you probably know that cannabis is mainly valued for two of its qualities: the "high" or "buzz" that's produced when you ingest it, and its healing qualities, such as its ability to relieve pain, diminish nausea, and prevent muscle spasms. But what produces these effects? To answer that question, we'll need to embark on a short chemistry lesson. Knowing what's in cannabis will help you choose the cannabis strain that's right for you—and it'll help you tune in to your body's reactions to it.

First of all, there are three different species of the cannabis plant: cannabis sativa, cannabis indica, and cannabis ruderalis. Sativa and indica are the best-known varieties, and most cannabis strains cultivated by growers are usually one or the other, or a hybrid of both. While there are nearly 500 known chemical compounds (or cannabinoids) in cannabis, the best-known are delta-9-tetrahydrocannibinol (THC) and cannabidiol (CBD).

THC is the psychoactive component in cannabis, which means it's responsible for the euphoria or "buzz" lots of folks experience when they consume it. But that's not all it's good for. Recent studies have shown that THC may be helpful in treating a number of medical conditions. It's been known to relieve vomiting or lack of appetite in cancer patients (it's a powerful antiemetic, and has even been said to relieve seasickness!) And, as a 2011 article published in the *British Journal of Clinical Pharmacology* shows, because THC binds to cannabinoid receptors in the central nervous system and the immune system, it can be effective in reducing symptoms like chronic pain in people with rheumatoid arthritis and fibromyalgia, among other conditions. Researchers have also begun to investigate its potential to prevent or treat some autoimmune and degenerative diseases: a 2009 article published in the medical journal *CNS: Neuroscience and Therapeutics* suggests that the anti-inflammatory properties of cannabis may halt the progression of neurodegeneration and minimize the neurological effects of stroke.

**CURB YOUR ENTHUSIASM.**

DON'T GET TOO CARRIED AWAY WHEN YOU'RE SAMPLING YOUR HOMEMADE CANNABIS COCKTAILS. ENJOY THEM SLOWLY, AND ALWAYS WAIT AT LEAST AN HOUR BETWEEN DRINKS. (WHAT'LL HAPPEN IF YOU DON'T? YOU'LL FEEL AS IF YOU WERE ON A CARNIVAL RIDE FROM HELL.) BUT SERIOUSLY, KEEP AN EYE ON YOUR PHYSICAL REACTIONS, AND STOP DRINKING IF YOU NOTICE YOU'RE NOT FEELING WELL.

CANNABIS CONNOISSEURSHIP

The potential medical benefits of THC are impressive, but CBD may possess even more possibilities for healing. Unlike THC, CBD is non-psychoactive, which means it doesn't make the user feel high or "stoned." And since that means fewer side effects, health professionals tend to prefer cannabis strains that are CBD-rich over those that are high in THC. Like its fellow cannabinoid THC, CBD has been shown to reduce nausea and vomiting and to suppress seizures. Thanks to these potential benefits, some growers have begun to produce strains that are very low in THC but high in CBD, so consumers can enjoy its healing properties minus the buzz.

Now that you know why ingesting cannabis gives you a high and why it's useful for a number of medical reasons, you're probably wondering what's responsible for its taste. The answer is terpenes. These are the compounds that give cannabis its distinctive tastes and scents. Produced by a wide variety of plants (and even by some insects!), terpenes are aromatic organic compounds that evaporate easily, and that are often strong-smelling. (It's no surprise that terpenes form the basis of aromatherapy, since they're found in the essential oils produced from plants and flowers.)

Cannabis contains about 200 different terpenes, some of which are being researched for their healing potential. Decarboxylation of cannabis—"decarbing" for short—releases these aromatic oils. You'll notice scents and flavors such as pine or resin, citrus fruits, roasted nuts, exotic spices, and sometimes—but not always—that traditional "skunky" fragrance. (You'll learn how, and why, to decarb your cannabis in chapter 3.)

In addition to levels of THC versus CBD, terpenes are also partly responsible for the physiological effects of the two main strains of cannabis. In general, *Cannabis sativa*, which is lower in THC, produces a "cerebral" high, promoting mental clarity and focus. You might find it more suitable for daytime use. *Cannabis indica*, on the other hand, is higher in THC and also contains more CBD, or cannabidiol, a component in cannabis which promotes sleep. This encourages full-body relaxation, so it may be better for evening use. Growers have created hundreds, if not thousands, of Sativa-Indica hybrids, which are bred to contain different quantities of these compounds, depending on their customers' needs: some offer high THC levels and lower CBD levels, or vice versa, while others aim for a balance of both.

# *Flavor Profiles of Different Cannabis Strains*

**Now that we've gotten our chemistry lesson out of the way, let's turn our attention to the scents and flavors that make each cannabis varietal unique. To date, thousands of strains of cannabis have been cultivated, and new ones are being developed so quickly that it seems as if there's a new one on the market every day. Here's a brief guide—complete with tasting notes—to some of the best-known strains: I've included some of my personal favorites, too.**

STRAIN: Blue Dream

FLAVOR PROFILE:

I'm a big fan of Blue Dream, which is actually a combination of two strains: indica-based Blueberry and sativa-based Haze. Lots of folks notice its aromas and flavors of sweet blue fruits—although I'm more attuned to its spiciness and its burnt-sugar overtones, which means it's wonderful in a hot toddy or when it's woven into the condensed milk in a cool Vietnamese-style iced coffee, like the one on page 52. Expect to feel relaxed yet clear-headed after enjoying it.

| MIXES WELL WITH: | BEST TIME OF THE DAY TO USE IT: |
|---|---|
| Bourbon, Scotch, and well-aged rum. | Evening, or whenever you're ready for deep, full-body relaxation. |

STRAIN: Maui Waui (or Maui Wowie)

FLAVOR PROFILE:

As its name suggests, Maui Waui hails from Hawaii, and it's redolent of freshly sliced honeydew melon, juicy navel oranges, tart lemons, and crushed pine needles. It's a sativa strain, and it's a versatile addition to cocktails with dominant flavors of citrus and spice. Weave it into a simple syrup or turn it into a tincture, and add it to a Ramos Gin Fizz. Deeply medicating.

| MIXES WELL WITH: | BEST TIME OF THE DAY TO USE IT: |
|---|---|
| Gin, vermouth, seltzer, freshly-squeezed juices, muddled grilled melon. | Late evening before bed, when it's time to wind down and calm your thoughts. |

STRAIN: OG Kush

FLAVOR PROFILE:

OG means Original Gangster, and sativa OG Kush is widely considered to be the original high-grade sensimilla strain. It's got a distinctive, piney scent, and its taste is clarifying and intense—just the thing to mix into a tincture and add to a mimosa made with freshly-squeezed blood oranges, or a refreshing glass of Moroccan-style mint tea, like the Honey Duke Relaxer on page 126.

| MIXES WELL WITH: | BEST TIME OF THE DAY TO USE IT: |
|---|---|
| Clear spirits like vodka and gin, and freshly squeezed citrus juices. | Daytime: try it in a brunch mocktail or cocktail. |

**STRAIN:** Thin Mint Cookie

**FLAVOR PROFILE:**

You won't believe that there's no cookie batter or mint chocolate chip ice cream in this hybrid sativa/indica strain. It's bursting with sweet, spicy notes that make it reminiscent of the Girl Scout Cookies strain, which may be its ancestor. Infuse a great bottle of Barr Hill gin with Thin Mint Cookie—the honey notes in the gin marry so well with the sweet earthiness of the Thin Mint—then mix yourself a minty, medicated gin and tonic. Or, use Thin Mint to make a batch of Canna-Butter, and add a pat to a homemade hot chocolate (for an extra treat, top it with a whisper of 160-proof rum and stir with a candy cane or peppermint stick). Alternatively, since Thin Mint may reduce nausea, you could always turn it into a tincture, then add a couple drops to a small bottle of aromatic bitters—after all, bitters have been used to remedy stomach ailments for centuries.

| MIXES WELL WITH: | BEST TIME OF THE DAY TO USE IT: |
|---|---|
| Rum, Scotch, bourbon, sweet vermouth, barrel-aged gin, botanical gin, and—in a pinch—vodka | This versatile strain can be used either during the day or at night: follow the advice of your caregiver. |

**STRAIN:** Sour Diesel

**FLAVOR PROFILE:**

Sour Diesel has a pungent aroma, like gasoline—but don't let that put you off. This sativa strain is marvelous when it's woven into an absinthe frappe, which consists of freshly crushed ice, absinthe, a little Sour Diesel–infused simple syrup, and crushed mint leaves. Toss all of the above into your Boston shaker until frosty, then sit back, relax, and put on some chamber music: everything feels more spacious after you've medicated with Sour Diesel. Although it's not the best remedy for deep body pain, some say it does a very good job of keeping stress and anxiety at bay.

| MIXES WELL WITH: | BEST TIME OF THE DAY TO USE IT: |
|---|---|
| Aged rum, Scotch, bourbon, rye, absinthe, gin and all types of vermouth. | Early in the morning and late afternoon or early evening |

**STRAIN:** Chocolate Chunk

**FLAVOR PROFILE:**

No, Virginia, there is no chocolate in this richly-textured indica strain. But there sure is a concentrated aroma of bittersweet chocolate that makes quite a statement. Try making a Chocolate Chunk tincture and infusing it in the Medicated Rich Simple Syrup (raw honey version) on page 43. Then, add it to a cup of looseleaf tea made with smoky lapsang souchong and a touch of citrusy Earl Grey. The result is reminiscent of dark chocolate-enrobed oranges, and it's heavenly.

| MIXES WELL WITH: | BEST TIME OF THE DAY TO USE IT: |
|---|---|
| Rum, chocolate liqueur, orange liqueur, mezcal, tequila, freshly-squeezed citrus juices, infused seltzer, and hot chocolate. | Daytime and evening |

**STRAIN:** Trainwreck

**FLAVOR PROFILE:**

It's hard to describe the taste of this unique hybrid strain, but here goes: Imagine pumpernickel toast smeared with French butter, then blanketed with Maine smoked salmon, and topped off with a dash of freshly ground white pepper—and you're pretty much there. It's this savoriness that makes it such a great addition to my version of the Bloody Caesar cocktail (a Canadian interpretation of the Bloody Mary) on page 134. Ready for a dose of couch-lock—when you're so relaxed that you're sure you're going to melt right into your couch? Then Trainwreck's just what you're looking for.

**MIXES WELL WITH:**

Cognac, rum, bourbon, vermouth, mezcal, tequila, barrel-aged gin, Canna-Butter, even a virgin milkshake

**BEST TIME OF THE DAY TO USE IT:**

Afternoon and evening

**STRAIN:** BC Bud

**FLAVOR PROFILE:**

Home, for this mostly Sativa hybrid, is British Columbia, and it's best enjoyed at the source. But if that's not doable, never fear. I've been consistently impressed with BC Bud and its smooth, funky flavor whenever (and wherever) I've tried it. It's as sweet as candy on the nose, but not on the finish, where you'll get gobs of freshly crushed Caribbean spices, fire-driven Thai spices, wet stones, and charred cedar. BC Bud is just gorgeous when it's whipped into a mixture of butter and coconut oil, and when it's fused into a glycerin tincture: both seem to magnify its fragrance and taste (not to mention its potency) a hundredfold. Add it to apple ice wine or a Sorel liqueur, such as the one by my friend Jack From Brooklyn (jackfrombrooklyn.com).

**MIXES WELL WITH:**

Belgian abbey beers, German wheat beers, hot chocolate, digestives, gin, vodka, bourbon, Scotch, seltzer, bitters and shrubs of all sorts

**BEST TIME OF THE DAY TO USE IT:**

Daytime and evening

**STRAIN:** Pineapple Kush

**FLAVOR PROFILE:**

Pineapple, mint, and burnt sugar meet in this mostly Indica strain. Turn it into a tincture or mix it into a batch of Canna-Butter (see page 44), and use it to medicate a hot cup of chamomile tea. It can alleviate muscle spasms, and may ease symptoms of stress and sleep disorders. In my experience, it'll send even the most ardent somnambulist straight to the Land of Nod. As for cocktails, you can't do better than adding a Pineapple Kush—infused orgeat syrup to a zombie: combine it with freshly squeezed orange and grapefruit juices, and a little bit of both light and dark rum.

**MIXES WELL WITH:**

After-dinner drinks (well-aged rum, cognac, or whiskies); tiki-bar-style preparations of all kinds (zombies and punches)

**BEST TIME OF THE DAY TO USE IT:**

Late evening

# 03

## YOUR CANNABIS PANTRY:
### *Tonics, Syrups, Shrubs, Tinctures, and Much More*

Before you start making handcrafted cannabis-infused cocktails, you'll need to make sure your pantry is properly stocked. This chapter will show you how to do just that. First, you'll find out what decarbolization is, and how to decarb your cannabis at home. Then, you'll learn how to safely make alcohol-based tinctures and infusions, plus compound butters, infused syrups, cannabis-laced shrubs, and more—and you'll learn safe ways to infuse spirits with cannabis, too.

# "Decarbing" Your Cannabis

Stop right there. Don't whip out those bottles of overproof rum and start stuffing bunches of raw cannabis into them. Before you use cannabis in preparations (such as infusions, syrups, tonics, and butters), you're probably going to want to decarboxylate it first. Decarboxylation is a chemical reaction that transforms tetrahydrocannabinolic acid (THCA)—a non-psychoactive compound in cannabis—into psychoactive tetrahydrocannabinol (THC). Chemically, this occurs when cannabis is gently heated or dried: the heating process releases the carbon dioxide molecule in THCA to produce THC. This process occurs naturally when you're smoking cannabis because smoking it involves applying heat to it.

## Why Decarb Your Cannabis?

There are two reasons for decarbing cannabis. First, decarbing is necessary to create the buzz that some people hope to achieve when they consume cannabis. If you don't decarb, you won't get the same buzz. Second, decarbing enhances the flavor of cannabis in the same way that toasting or dry-frying nuts or spices coaxes out their hidden flavors. The spicy quality inherent in raw cannabis disappears, and different aromatics take its place thanks to cannabis's terpenes (the compounds I mentioned in chapter 2).

You can even decarb regular garden-variety herbs to make your own infused oils and vinegars: the process works the same way for all kinds of plant material.

That said, you might not be in the market for the buzz that the psychoactive THC in decarbed cannabis yields—and that's fine. If that's the case, you don't need to decarb your cannabis. Raw cannabis still contains CBD and THCA, and THC's parent compound has similar health benefits to THC. Essentially, non-decarbed cannabis will have the same healing properties you read about in chapter 2, including pain relief: the only difference is, you won't get high from it.

## Basic Decarb Techniques

Decarbing your cannabis is simple. There are two ways to do it at home: baking it in the oven, or boiling it in a saucepan on your stove top. There's no difference in the end result. Both methods will leave you with decarbed cannabis that's ready for use in your preparations. Since it doesn't involve toasting or baking, the boiling (or *sous vide*) method will produce less of a smell, so you might want to opt for it if you have nosy neighbors next door.

## Oven method

Preheat the oven to 250°F (120°C, or gas mark 1/2). For extra accuracy regarding oven temperature, use an oven thermometer. Grind 1 to 2 ounces (28 to 56 g) cannabis flowers in a clean metal grinder, such as a coffee grinder. Spread the ground cannabis evenly into an ovenproof glass or cast-iron pan with an airtight lid. Alternatively, spread it evenly in an aluminum pie tin and cover tightly with several layers of aluminum foil.

Place the pan in the oven and bake for 30 minutes, or until the buds are golden brown. Be forewarned: your kitchen will smell strongly of toasted cannabis! So, be sure to cover the pan very tightly. Use several fans to air out your workspace, if necessary, or decarb outdoors using a covered toaster oven. Do not open your oven while the cannabis is cooking, if you can help it: this may interrupt the decarbing process.

After your cannabis has rested for 15 minutes, it's ready to use in preparations such as butters, oils, syrups, and tinctures.

**PRO-TIP**: LET THE CANNABIS COOL FOR 15 MINUTES BEFORE REMOVING THE LID OR THE FOIL COVER: THIS ALLOWS THE TERPENES, OR FRAGRANT AROMATICS, TO SEEP BACK INTO THE DECARBED CANNABIS—JUST LIKE YOU'D LET MEAT OR POULTRY "REST" BEFORE SLICING OR SERVING IT. YOU DON'T WANT TO LOSE THOSE WONDERFUL AROMAS OF PINE, TROPICAL FRUITS, MINT, CITRUS, AND SPICES.

**DON'T KICK UP THE HEAT.** YOU SHOULD ALWAYS DECARB YOUR CANNABIS IN A CLOSED CONTAINER AT A QUITE LOW TEMPERATURE: THAT IS, BELOW 300°F (150°C). OTHERWISE, THOSE VOLATILE TERPENES WILL EVAPORATE, AND THAT CAN HAPPEN ALL TOO QUICKLY. SO PAY ATTENTION TO THE CLOCK—AND TO YOUR NOSE! YOU'LL KNOW THAT IT'S TIME TO TAKE YOUR CANNABIS OUT OF THE OVEN AND LET IT REST WHEN IT REALLY STARTS TO SMELL STRONGLY.

## Boiling, or *sous vide*, method

*Sous vide* means "in a vacuum" in French, and that's exactly how this method works: you'll boil your cannabis in a "vacuum" in a heat-proof pouch, just as if you were making instant rice. And it's just as easy as the oven method. Here's how to do it:

Bring a large saucepan of water to a simmer (approximately 200°F, or 93°C). Place the whole cannabis flowers into a boilable cooking pouch. Seal the packet well so that it's airtight. Add the pouch to the water, and simmer for 90 minutes, keeping an eye on the water level so that it doesn't run too low. If necessary, add boiling water to ensure the bag is submerged. Remove the bag from the water, and let it cool for 10 to 15 minutes before opening and using in your preparations.

THE ONE-HOUR RULE. REMEMBER THAT THE EFFECTS OF CONSUMING THC-ACTIVATED CANNABIS WILL TAKE ABOUT AN HOUR TO KICK IN, SO PLEASE PLAN ACCORDINGLY. CLEAR YOUR SCHEDULE. MAKE SURE THAT YOU DON'T NEED TO DRIVE. AND EVEN IF YOU'RE ACCUSTOMED TO HAVING MORE THAN ONE DRINK IN AN HOUR, BE SURE TO WAIT TO SEE WHAT EFFECT THE DRINK HAS ON YOU BEFORE YOU EVEN THINK ABOUT HAVING ANOTHER.

Sous vide methc
one of seve
decarb techniqu

# Making Cannabis Infusions and Tinctures

Now that you know how to decarb your cannabis, you can start turning it into infusions and tinctures. Technically, you don't have to decarb before adding cannabis to infusions. I always decarb my cannabis, and that's reflected in these recipes, but do feel free to use raw cannabis if you like. Remember that different strains of cannabis have different levels of CBD and THC, so ask your caregiver whether or not you should decarb before making infusions and tinctures.

NEVER USE ALCOHOL WITH A GAS STOVE. REMEMBER THAT ALCOHOL IS FLAMMABLE AND CAN BE HIGHLY VOLATILE IF YOU'RE NOT CAREFUL. KEEP ALCOHOL AWAY FROM GAS STOVES AND OPEN FLAMES, AND MAKE SURE YOUR WORKSPACE IS WELL VENTILATED.

Add ground, decarbed cannabis directly into liquor always in a double boiler.

As an alternative method of infusion, add cannabis and any flavorings to a cheesecloth pouch.

Carefully pour your infused liquor into your choice of bottles.

## Infusions

To make a cannabis infusion, add 7 grams—or the dosage recommended by your caregiver—of ground, decarbed cannabis to 250 ml (about 1 cup) of a liquor of your choice in a heat-proof mason jar. **Do not seal the jar, it could burst.** Place the jar in the top of a double boiler on a hot plate or electric stove top.

(Never, ever use a gas stove or an open flame.) Fill the top of the double boiler with enough water to cover the mason jar halfway.

Simmer lightly at around 160°F (71°C) for 30 to 60 minutes. Use a digital thermometer to keep an eye on the temperature. Alcohol flames just over 170°F (77°C), so pay close attention to the job at hand, and don't go running out for a pizza. Plus, a low heat will keep evaporation to a minimum.

Let the mixture cool, strain it through a fine-mesh strainer lined with cheesecloth, then funnel it back into the empty liquor bottle. Top up the bottle with the remaining un-infused liquor until it's back to a volume of 750 ml. This ensures that the THC will be dispersed throughout the infusion. Your infusion is now ready to use in your handcrafted cocktails.

BITTERS AND CANNABIS. BITTERS ARE A CONCENTRATED CURATIVE MADE FROM BOTANICALS LIKE ROOTS, BARK, AND SPICES. THEY'VE BEEN USED IN EUROPEAN FOLK MEDICINE SINCE THE SIXTEENTH CENTURY. WITH THEIR HIGH ALCOHOL CONTENT AND GUT-FRIENDLY HERBS AND SPICES, BITTERS WERE SOMETIMES USED TO PURIFY WATER AND TO TREAT DEBILITATING BELLY-RELATED AILMENTS. (A TEASPOON OF BITTERS MIXED INTO A GLASS OF SELTZER WATER CAN BE HELPFUL IN RELIEVING GASTRIC DISTRESS—INCLUDING MOTION SICK-NESS.) STOMACH-SOOTHING CANNABIS WOULD HAVE CERTAINLY FEATURED IN APOTHECARY-PREPARED BITTERS IN THE DAYS BEFORE REFRIGERATION AND MODERN FOOD PRESERVATION METHODS. THESE DAYS, ADDING CAN-NABIS TINCTURES TO YOUR FAVORITE BITTERS LENDS BALANCE, DEPTH, AND SYNERGY TO CRAFT COCKTAILS—AND, DEPENDING ON THE STRAIN AND THC OR CBD CONTENT, MAY BE ABLE TO OFFER RELIEF FOR CHRONIC PAIN, TOO.

## Tinctures

A tincture is a much more concentrated version of an infusion. Tinctures can be used in cocktails, but you can also self-medicate—in accordance with your caregiver's instructions, of course—by placing a drop or two under your tongue. And, unlike infusions, they're frequently made with raw cannabis.

Here's how to make one: Follow the instructions for making an infusion, but use raw cannabis, if you like. Cook the cannabis-alcohol mixture for another 4 hours over a very low heat, until the liquid has been reduced by about three-quarters. Watch it closely to make sure the liquid doesn't evaporate completely, leaving you with nothing but your (expensive) dreams. Keep your workspace well ventilated when you're making a tincture: they tend to produce a strong aroma. Tinctures are powerful in terms of both taste and physical effect, but they're much lower in alcohol than infusions, which makes them great additions to mocktails.

In the following pages, I'll introduce you to some of my own recipes for infusions, butters, oils, and lots more.

MAKING TINCTURES WITH A MAGICAL BUTTER MACHINE. IF YOU'RE PLANNING TO MAKE CANNABIS TINCTURES FREQUENTLY, YOU MIGHT WANT TO INVEST IN A MAGICAL BUTTER MACHINE (MAGICALBUTTER.COM). IT DOES ALL THE HARD WORK FOR YOU: ALL YOU NEED TO DO IS STAY NEARBY DURING THE PROCESS. HERE'S HOW IT WORKS. ADD 2 CUPS (475 ML) OF LIQUOR OF YOUR CHOICE TO THE MACHINE, THEN ADD 1 OUNCE (28 G) DECARBED CANNABIS. SET THE TEMPERATURE TO 160°F (71°C) AND PRESS THE "4 HOUR TINCTURE" BUTTON. THE MACHINE WILL PULVERIZE THE CANNABIS, GENTLY HEAT IT TO 160°F (71°C), AND WILL SLOWLY REDUCE THE LIQUID IN THE SAME WAY YOU'D DO IT BY HAND AT THE STOVE.

# Infused Absinthe

My Infused Absinthe is my own take on the classic—and potent—Green Dragon tincture, and it turns up in many of the cocktails in this book. Choose a quality absinthe—and, before you berate me for adulterating an excellent bottle of absinthe with cannabis, let me remind you that cannabis found its way into just about every kind of alcohol in the late nineteenth and early twentieth centuries. Given its popularity, there's nothing to suggest that absinthe missed the party. So, get out your hot plate (or your Magical Butter Machine), and add a dose of cannabis to the Green Fairy.

## INGREDIENTS

· 8 GRAMS GROUND, DECARBED CANNABIS

· 250 ML ABSINTHE, JADE LIQUEURS' ESPRIT EDOUARD

Combine the cannabis and absinthe into a large, heatproof mason jar. Do not seal the jar. I repeat. Do not seal it; it could burst. Place the jar in the top of a double boiler set on an electric stove or hot plate. Heat the bottom of the boiler to 200°F (93°C). The top of the boiler, filled halfway up the sides of the canning jar, should not exceed 160°F (71°C). Simmer for 60 minutes at 160°F (71°C). Use a digital thermometer to keep an eye on the temperature. Do not let the pot run dry! Stir the absinthe often, and be sure to work in a well-ventilated space. Cool completely, then reconstitute the infused absinthe with fresh absinthe from the bottle to bring up to your desired level.

Alternatively, you can make this infusion using the Magical Butter Machine. (No need to grind the cannabis.) Add the cannabis and liquor to the Magical Butter Machine, set the temperature to 160°F (71°C) and the timer to 2 hours.

# Cannabis Cream or Milk

If you think you can't live without your morning coffee, just wait until you've tried topping off your cup of joe with a tablespoon or two of this luscious cannabis-infused cream. It's really easy to make, and it's practically guaranteed to turn you into a morning person. Make it with your favorite Sativa strain. Sativas are ideal for morning use because they promote wakefulness and clear thinking. Just remember to skip the skim milk: the result won't be nearly as good if you don't use full-fat milk or cream, which have plenty of butterfat.

## INGREDIENTS

- 1 CUP (235 ML) HEAVY CREAM, LIGHT CREAM, HALF-AND-HALF, OR WHOLE MILK
- 1 GRAM GROUND, DECARBED CANNABIS
- 1 TEASPOON VANILLA EXTRACT OR DARK RUM (OR 1/2 TEASPOON OF EACH)

Add the cream and ground cannabis to a small saucepan and heat until just below boiling, about 160°F (71°C). Measure the heat carefully with a heat-proof candy thermometer. (Don't have one? Now's the time to invest!) Scrape off any film that appears on the sides of the saucepan. Stir constantly to avoid burning.

Add the vanilla or rum, then turn down the heat and cover the saucepan with a lid. Continue to cook on a very low heat for 1 hour, stirring frequently. Do not boil. Strain the mixture through cheesecloth into a bowl, squeezing out as much liquid as possible. Use the infused cream in coffee and tea recipes or in THC-infused milk punches. Store in the fridge for up to 4 days.

# THC-Infused Condensed Milk

~~~

Westerners tend to reserve condensed milk for cooking, baking, or making confectionery, but there are plenty of other applications for it—many of them drinkable. You'll want to have a batch of this THC-Infused Condensed Milk on hand if you're planning to make the Cannabis-Infused Vietnamese Iced Coffee on page 52. It's also essential for the warming, coffee-based Potato Head Blues on page 116. And you don't have to stop there, either: go ahead and add a tablespoon or so to your favorite tea or coffee (hot or iced).

═══════════════ INGREDIENTS ═══════════════

· 1 CAN (8 OUNCES, OR 235 ML) SWEETENED CONDENSED MILK

· 3-4 GRAMS DECARBED CANNABIS, PLACED IN A HEMP TEA BAG

.....................................................

Add the condensed milk and ground cannabis to a small saucepan. Heat until just below boiling, about 165°F (74°C). Turn down the heat to low, and cook for 1 hour to infuse the condensed milk with the cannabis.

Remove the teabag, squeezing out as much of the condensed milk as possible. Transfer the mixture to a heat-proof bowl. The result will be very thick and concentrated. (That's a good thing!) Dilute it with fresh condensed milk until you've reached the desired consistency and volume. Let cool completely and use in recipes that include medicated condensed milk. Store in the fridge for 5 to 7 days.

# Canna-Coconut Oil

**This recipe calls for sunflower lecithin, which facilitates the absorption of THC: don't confuse it with soy lecithin, which is packed with GMOs.**

=== INGREDIENTS ===

· 6 GRAMS OF CANNABIS

· 2 CUPS (436 G) COCONUT OIL

· 4 TABLESPOONS (26 G) SUNFLOWER LECITHIN POWDER (OR 60 ML LIQUID)

...............................................

Decarb the cannabis for 45 minutes at 250°F (120°C). (See page 30)

Combine the oil and sunflower lecithin in a slow cooker set to the lowest setting. Melt slowly, and stir often. Add the cannabis, and stir every 15 minutes. After 4 to 5 hours, turn off the slow cooker and allow the mixture to cool slightly.

Line a strainer with two pieces of cheesecloth, and secure with a large rubber band. Place the strainer into a heat-proof container, then slowly pour the mixture into the strainer. Tighten the cheesecloth into a ball using a piece of string. Put on heat-proof gloves (it will still be quite warm), and squeeze the cheesecloth to extract any remaining oil.

Pour the oil into a sterilized pint jar, seal with a tight-fitting lid, and label it clearly. Store in fridge for up to 1 year.

# Canna-Coconut Cream

**How do you get the cannabis *into* the coconut cream? Happily, it's easier than it sounds. You only need two ingredients to make my Canna-Coconut Cream: a batch of the Canna-Coconut Oil (left), and plain cream of coconut. (Be sure to buy the sweetened, organic version.) Then, you "infuse" the liquefied oil into the coconut cream—and you're done.**

=== INGREDIENTS ===

· 2 OUNCES (54 G) CANNA-COCONUT OIL (SEE LEFT)

· 6 OUNCES (177 ML) CREAM OF COCONUT

...............................................

Place the cream of coconut in a bowl. Heat the Canna-Coconut Oil for about 15 seconds in the top of a double boiler, until it turns clear. Remove it from the heat, and add it to the cream of coconut. Mix well to combine, and use in recipes that call for coconut cream. You can even add it to a vegetable curry! Store in the fridge for up to 2 weeks.

# Canna-Maple Syrup

**Use this THC-infused maple syrup in my medicated maple syrup Sazerac (608 Bush Street on page 84)—or drizzle a little on your pancakes and bacon on a weekend morning.**

## INGREDIENTS

6 GRAMS GROUND, DECARBED CANNABIS

16 OUNCES (454 G) PURE MAPLE SYRUP

Divide the ground cannabis between several hemp tea bags. Fill a sterilized mason jar with the maple syrup and add the tea bags. Do not seal the jar. Place the jar in a double boiler fitted with a candy thermometer. Fill the top of the double boiler with enough water to cover the jar halfway. Heat the water in the double boiler to 170°F (77°C).

Reduce the temperature and simmer the mixture at about 160°F (71°C) for at least 4 hours, replacing water as necessary from both the bottom and top of the double boiler. Remove the jar from the double boiler and let cool overnight. Check to be sure the jar is well sealed, then shake well to combine.

Heat the water in the double boiler again to a very light simmer (about 170°F or 77°C). Return the jar to the double boiler, and simmer for another two hours. Cool completely, then strain the mixture through a cheesecloth-lined strainer.

If you like, try adding 1/2 cup (120 ml) of bourbon to the Canna-Maple Syrup, and age in a cool place (e.g., fridge or cellar) for 1 month before using.

**No-cook method: This method requires no heat, and makes a larger batch.** Alternatively, if you can get your hands on a 64-ounce (1.9 l) oak bourbon barrel, you can fill it with dark maple syrup, then add about 1/2 ounce of ground, decarbed cannabis in hemp tea bags. Store for about 1 month in a cool, dark place. Wearing rubber gloves, remove the cannabis tea bags and squeeze out any remaining syrup. Strain the syrup into sterilized bottles.

# Medicated Rich Simple Syrup

**Simple syrup is an essential weapon in any bartender's arsenal, and if you're making cannabis cocktails, you'll want to have a batch of this at the ready. Feel free to make it with either Demerara sugar or raw honey—and you can also doctor it up with just about any kind of fresh herb or flavoring. (The glycerine helps speed up the absorption of THC into your digestive system.) Use it in just about any recipe that calls for simple syrup.**

## INGREDIENTS

**If using Demerara sugar:**

· 1 CUP FILTERED SPRING WATER

· 1 CUP DEMERARA SUGAR

· 4 GRAMS FINELY GROUND
  DECARBED CANNABIS

· 1 TABLESPOON VEGETARIAN
  (NON-GMO) LIQUID LECITHIN

**If using raw honey:**

· 2 CUPS FILTERED SPRING WATER

· 1 CUP RAW HONEY

· 4 GRAMS FINELY GROUND
  DECARBED CANNABIS

· 1 TABLESPOON VEGETARIAN
  (NON-GMO) LIQUID LECITHIN

Pour the water into a saucepan and bring to a rolling boil. Reduce the temperature to about 190°F. Add the sugar or raw honey and stir it until it is completely dissolved into the water. (If you're using raw honey and you find that the syrup looks too clear, add a little more honey.) Add the cannabis, then cover the saucepan. Reduce the heat again to about 160°F and simmer for at least 30 minutes to infuse the simple syrup with the cannabis.

Reduce the temperature a third time, to medium-low, and add the lecithin. Cook for another 10 minutes, stirring constantly to prevent cooking and burning. Remove from the heat, and strain through a cheesecloth-lined strainer into a stainless steel bowl that's resting in a larger, ice-filled container. This will help it cool quickly. Makes about 1 cup.

To make a **Medicated Rich Ginger Simple Syrup**, make the Medicated Rich Simple Syrup with raw honey instead of sugar, and add a 1-inch piece of ginger root, peeled and thickly sliced, along with the cannabis. Continue with the recipe as directed.

# Canna-Butter, Two Ways

I use cannabis-infused, clarified butter—in all sorts of drinks, from cocktails and mocktails to coffee- and tea-based beverages. You can make it in a slow cooker for a larger batch or on the stove in a sauté pan for a smaller batch.

## INGREDIENTS

### Slow Cooker

· 1 LB. (4 STICKS, OR 450 G) UNSALTED, HIGH-FAT BUTTER, OR 1½ CUPS (360 ML) GHEE

· 1 OUNCE CANNABIS, GROUND ROUGHLY

### Stove Top

· 1 STICK (112 G) UNSALTED, HIGH-FAT BUTTER OR 1/3 CUP (80 ML) GHEE

· 1/4 OUNCE GROUND, DECARBED CANNABIS

· 2 TABLESPOONS (28 G) COCONUT OIL

Following the instructions on page 30, decarb the cannabis for 45 minutes at 240°F (116°C). Then let it rest covered for 15 minutes.

If you're using butter, clarify it first: Heat the butter in a medium saucepan until it's just simmering. Scoop off the white solids that appear on top of the melted butter, and discard.

Set your slow cooker to low. Combine the clarified butter and cannabis in the slow cooker, and heat very slowly for at least two hours. Let cool. Then, reheat for another hour or so at no more than 160°F (71°C). Simmer very lightly and do not boil. Strain the mixture through cheesecloth or a very fine-mesh stainless steel sieve.

Add the butter to a sauté pan, then add the cannabis. Cook on a low simmer for a minimum of 1 hour, stirring constantly. When the mixture stops bubbling, the butter is done and is fully medicated. Pour the Canna-Butter through a fine-mesh stainless steel sieve into a small pan, pressing down on the ground cannabis with a wooden spoon to squeeze out as much butter as possible. Use melted cannabis butter immediately in drinks. Alternatively, store for 1 week in the fridge, or 1 month in the freezer. Label the package clearly, and keep away from children.

# Quick Strawberry–Balsamic Canna–Shrub

**This THC-laced version takes just 48 hours to make, and it's delicious.**

=== INGREDIENTS ===

· 1 (8 OUNCE) JAR STRAWBERRY PRESERVES

· 8 OUNCES WHITE BALSAMIC VINEGAR

· 4 GRAMS GROUND, DECARBED CANNABIS PLACED IN A TISANE-TYPE TEA BAG

Add the preserves to the balsamic vinegar and stir well to combine. Add the cannabis. Heat the mixture in a double boiler at 160°F (71 °C) for 1 hour. Let cool.

Let the tisane rest in the mixture for at least 48 hours at cellar temperature (50-55°F [10-13°C]), or in the refrigerator, mixing well at intervals. Mash all the ingredients using a wooden spoon, then remove the tea bag, squeezing out as much liquid from it as possible. Strain through a fine-meshed sieve lined with cheesecloth. Discard the solids. Transfer the liquid to a sterilized jar, and use in your craft cocktails. Store in the fridge for up to 1 year.

# Greenish Cocktail Cherries

**I'm a bit of an evangelist when it comes to homemade cocktail cherries. They're far, far superior to those red things that come in jars.**

=== INGREDIENTS ===

· 1 BOTTLE (750 ML) OF BOURBON WHISKEY

· 8 GRAMS OF DECARBED CANNABIS

· 2 POUNDS (910 G) PITTED FRESH CHERRIES

Infuse the whiskey with the cannabis following the instructions on page 34. Place the pitted cherries in a large mason jar, then cover with the infused whiskey. Store the jar in a cool, dark place, such as a cellar or refrigerator, for 1 month, shaking the jar daily. Don't be afraid to store these outside the fridge at cellar temperature: nothing bad will happen if you do. Use as called for in cocktails and mocktails.

# PART II

# CANNABIS DRINKS

# 04

## THE GREAT BEGINNINGS

Not everyone is a morning person. Whether it's due to a bout of insomnia, chronic pain that just won't quit, or—less often, I hope—the aftereffects of a few too many whiskies, it can be tough to drag yourself out of bed at times. And when it comes to self-medication, do you really want to chew down heavy pot brownies for breakfast on a daily basis? Didn't think so. I wouldn't want to, either—which is why this chapter contains carefully-curated cocktails and mocktails that are delicious alternatives to cannabis-laden carbs.

### NOTE

ALL RECIPES MAKE ONE SERVING, UNLESS OTHERWISE NOTED

**B**ut that doesn't mean you should give breakfast a miss altogether. Before you enjoy the drinks in this chapter, it's important to eat something healthy and relatively substantial. (My dream breakfast is the classic American triumvirate of warm pancakes, crisp bacon, and a hot fried egg—but feel free to eat whatever sounds good to you.)

Unless your doctor tells you otherwise, it's usually a wise idea to make sure there's food in your stomach before taking pharmaceuticals of any kind—and the same goes for herbal medicinal preparations, including cannabis. Plus, having food in your stomach before you sip a cannabis cocktail or mocktail will help you absorb the nutrients in it, including the cannabinoids. And, after all, intoxication isn't our goal here. These drinks are meant to soothe and heal, so you won't want to overmedicate before your day has even begun.

Coffee, tea, and other milk-based cannabis-infused beverages are a great way to consume cannabis on the early side of the day. They're comforting and satisfying—and can be either warming or cooling, depending on your mood and what the weather's doing. And they're so much more interesting than that dreary cup of instant coffee you stir together halfheartedly first thing in the morning. Just as importantly, they taste wonderful, too.

For each recipe, I've suggested cannabis strains that work especially well with the drink's ingredients— keeping in mind, of course, that you'll probably want to try these in the a.m. You can experiment with different cannabis strains, if you like: just be sure to follow your caregiver's recommendations, because he or she will be well acquainted with your individual needs and your medical history. In general, Sativa strains promote focus and clarity, while Indica strains foster physical and mental relaxation, so do keep that in mind as you make the cocktails in this chapter.

Finally, whichever strains you choose, do remember that less is always more when it comes to cannabis: you don't have to consume your dosage for an entire day in a single sip. This isn't a horse race, so take your time, and sip slowly. Always, always, always wait at least an hour between drinks, so that you can keep an eye on your body's responses to them, and stop drinking right away if you don't feel well. Ultimately, the best way to savor the drinks in this chapter applies to just about every kind of human activity there is: Concentrate on being peaceful and patient, and enjoy each and every sip.

# Shake It, Sugaree

I love breakfast cocktails. Maybe that's because everything tastes better when your palate is open—before you've covered it up with lunch. One of the best breakfast cocktails I've ever had is a frozen Irish coffee. My version is simple to make—hardly more than crushed ice, cannabis-infused heavy whipping cream, and chilled strong coffee—but the result is so much greater than the sum of its parts. Try making your Cannabis Cream with an Indica strain, like Holy Grail Kush: it's spicy and savory, and complements the toasty notes of the Irish whiskey like a pro. To make a nonalcoholic version, turn the Shake It, Sugaree into a medicated egg cream: just skip the whiskey and brandy, add a squirt of chocolate syrup, and top with a few ounces of soda water after blending.

## INGREDIENTS

- 2 OUNCES (60 ML) CANNABIS CREAM (SEE PAGE 39), MADE WITH HEAVY WHIPPING CREAM
- 1 SCOOP COFFEE ICE CREAM
- 1/2 OUNCE (15 ML) IRISH WHISKEY
- 1/2 OUNCE (15 ML) BRANDY
- 1 TEASPOON PURE VANILLA EXTRACT
- 3 OUNCES (90 ML) BREWED ESPRESSO COFFEE, COOLED
- 1 CUP ICE

Simply combine all ingredients in a blender, and blend until they are well incorporated. Serve in a tall glass. Straws optional.

# Cannabis-Infused Condensed Milk & Vietnamese Coffee (Cân Sa Và Cà Phê)

Cold, Vietnamese-style coffee, with its sweet, unctuous condensed milk, offers nothing less than full-body gratification. Now you can make a medicated version at home: the key is the THC-Infused Condensed Milk on page 40. For this recipe, try making it with an Indica strain, like Blueberry: its fruity aromatics are a beautiful match for the chicory coffee. Darkly-flavored Fire OG, also a Sativa, works well here, too. If you need a quick fix, skip the lengthy heating process involved in making infused condensed milk, and add no more than 10 ml of an Indica tincture to regular condensed milk before using it in your cocktail. Couch-lock will result, so don't be tempted to have more than one of these—and be sure to stay away from cars, bicycles, and anything else with wheels until the effects of your Cân sa và cà phê have worn off.

## INGREDIENTS

- COCONUT WATER ICE CUBES
- 2 OUNCES (60 ML) THC-INFUSED CONDENSED MILK (SEE PAGE 40)
- 1 TEASPOON POWDERED LECITHIN
- 6 OUNCES (180 ML) VIETNAMESE-STYLE CHICORY COFFEE, COOLED
- MORE COCONUT WATER ICE CUBES, CRUSHED (OPTIONAL)

Add the coconut water ice cubes to a tall glass. Pour in the condensed milk, then stir in the lecithin. Top with the chicory coffee. Top with the crushed coconut water ice cubes, if desired. Stir, and serve immediately.

# Beside the Bosphorus

Making good Turkish coffee is nothing like making typical American-style percolated coffee, which is, far too often, short on flavor and character. Preparing thick, plush Turkish coffee requires time and patience—and it's worth every second. Try using Egyptian or Lebanese Turkish-style coffee, which has cardamom seeds pre-ground into the mix. I like my Turkish coffee medium sweet, just like James Bond: if you do, too, add the sugar to the ibrik before brewing the coffee. Toasting the sugar for a few seconds over an open flame lends it a rich, caramel-tinged finish. Just before serving, you'll want to top it with a pat of Canna-Butter infused with an Indica strain, such as Gorilla Glue: its aromatics of exotic spices match well with the cardamom-laced coffee, and it's suitable for either day or evening uses. This drink was created for my friend Joy Stocke, who inspired me with her lush descriptions of Turkey.

## INGREDIENTS

· 1 TEASPOON DEMERARA SUGAR OR RAW SUGAR

· 1 TABLESPOON (15 G) TURKISH COFFEE

· 1-2 OUNCES (30-60 ML) COOL WATER

· 1 TEASPOON CANNA-BUTTER (SEE PAGE 44)

Add the Demerara sugar and Turkish coffee to an ibrik. Toast over a low flame for 15 seconds in order to caramelize the sugar; this adds a toasty note to the coffee. Add the water. Bring to a simmer, and remove from the heat just before it boils over. Repeat 2 to 3 times. Be patient: this process is essential to making good Turkish coffee! Pour the coffee into a demitasse cup, top with the Canna-Butter: let it melt into the coffee for a moment. Then sip slowly and thoughtfully. Wait at least an hour before having another.

# Hot Spiced Apple Cider for a (Small) Crowd

Is there anything better than a mug of hot apple cider on a crisp fall day? Yes, sir, there is: a mug of hot apple cider that you've dosed with cannabis-infused whiskey and topped with a honeyed, medicated whipped cream that melts into the warm cider as you sip it. Use a whiskey that you've infused with an Indica strain, such as Blue Dream: it's wonderfully relaxing, and tastes like sugar-coated fresh blueberries—and, somehow, like the aromatics in chai tea.

## INGREDIENTS

- 16 OUNCES (475 ML) HOT APPLE CIDER (MADE FROM LOCALLY-SOURCED ORGANIC APPLES, IF POSSIBLE)

- ASSORTED BAKING SPICES OF YOUR CHOICE (SUCH AS CINNAMON, CLOVES, CARDAMOM, OR EVEN CURRY POWDER), MUDDLED TOGETHER WITH A MORTAR AND PESTLE

- 2 OUNCES (60 ML) MEDICATED RICH SIMPLE SYRUP (SEE PAGE 43), MADE WITH RAW HONEY

- 2 CUPS (475 ML) HEAVY WHIPPING CREAM

- 1½ OUNCES (45 ML) CANNABIS-INFUSED BARRELL WHISKEY

- SPRINKLE OF SEA SALT

- LIGHT SPRINKLE OF THAI-STYLE CHILI POWDER

Combine the apple cider and baking spices in a medium saucepan. Heat gently until warmed through.

In a nonreactive container, whisk the Medicated Rich Simple Syrup with the heavy whipping cream until soft peaks form.

Divide the hot apple cider between preheated mugs, add the Barrell whiskey, and top each with a dollop of the whipping cream mixture. Sprinkle each with a bit of sea salt and a very small pinch of chili powder. (Be careful: more than a touch will make it too spicy!) Serve immediately.

SERVES 5 TO 7

# Drinking in New Delhi

**Chai tea, as a rule, consists of a splendid and diverse mixture of spices, including cinnamon, cardamom, cloves, and black pepper. Each of these spices has its own set of healing properties within traditional Asian medicine—cloves, for instance, can act as an analgesic, and can aid digestive health. When you add a cannabis tincture to the mix, the result is a warming libation that's really soothing, relaxing, and deeply medicated. Use a South Asian Indica strain in this drink: its smoky-sweet flavors meld beautifully with the milky tea.**

## INGREDIENTS

- 1 CUP (235 ML) MILK OR CREAM

- 1 TABLESPOON (7 G) EACH CINNAMON, CARDAMOM, CLOVES, BLACK PEPPERCORNS AND GROUND GINGER, LIGHTLY CRUSHED TOGETHER WITH A STONE MORTAR AND PESTLE, THEN PLACED IN A HEMP TEABAG

- 1-2 GRAMS DECARBED CANNABIS, PLACED IN A SEPARATE HEMP TEABAG

- 2 TABLESPOONS (4 G) LOOSE LEAF BLACK CHINESE TEA

- 2 TABLESPOONS (40 G) RAW HONEY OR RAW SUGAR

- 1 TEASPOON NON-MEDICATED SWEET BUTTER, TO FINISH

Place the milk in a small saucepan. Add the teabags with the spices and cannabis, and heat at 160°F (71°C) for 1 hour, stirring frequently to prevent a film from forming on the milk. Use a heat-proof kitchen thermometer to make sure that the heat does not exceed 160°F (71°C). Remove the teabags and discard. In a separate saucepan, brew the tea to the desired strength, then fold in the milk mixture and combine gently. Stir in the honey. Serve in your favorite handcrafted tea cups, and top each with 1/2 teaspoon of butter.

SERVES 2

# No One Can Talk to a Horse, Of Course

If you're a purist when it comes to martinis—which is only fitting and proper, after all—you probably blanch at the loathsome words "chocolate martini," which is why I've named this drink something completely outré. Keep calm: while it does involve chocolate, this cocktail bears no resemblance to those awful vodka-based concoctions you find in way too many overpriced bars. Instead, it calls for cannabis-infused Barrell bourbon (barrellbourbon.com)— but if you haven't got it on hand, go ahead and make your infusion with any quality bourbon of your choice. As for the cannabis, try the Chocolate Chunk strain: it's got deep chocolate notes interwoven with aromatics of pungent soil and crushed tree bark. And, as with all cannabis cocktails, remember to enjoy it slowly and mindfully.

## INGREDIENTS

- 2 OUNCES (60 ML) GOOD-QUALITY CHOCOLATE SYRUP
- 1 OUNCE (30 ML) CANNABIS-INFUSED BARRELL BOURBON WHISKEY
- 2 OUNCES (60 ML) CHOCOLATE LIQUEUR
- FRESHLY WHIPPED CREAM, TO SERVE
- SHAVED DARK CHOCOLATE (MINIMUM 70% COCOA SOLIDS), FOR GARNISH
- ICE

Fill a mixing glass two-thirds full with ice. Add the chocolate syrup, bourbon, and chocolate liqueur. Mix well and pour into a prechilled martini glass. Top with a dollop of whipped cream and shave a little dark chocolate over the top to finish. Serve with two short straws.

# King Tubby's Dub Song

This cocktail bears a passing resemblance to the piña colada, that well-known work-horse of the booze-cruise—except King Tubby's Dub Song is far better. (Let's not even talk about those pseudo-coladas that are made from premixed concentrate.) King Tubby's features grilled pineapple juice, a moderate dose of rum, and a lick of orgeat syrup, which tastes like almonds and orange-flower water. Then it's given a dose of physic in the form of luxurious Canna-Coconut Cream. Try making yours with the OG Kush strain: its unique aromatics of lemon zest and diesel fuel add nuance to the tropical flavors of the Tubby. (By the way, the scent of diesel fuel may sound undesirable, but it's actually a good thing: it's an indicator of high-quality terpenes.) Then put down your smartphone, and head off on an hour-long staycation.

## INGREDIENTS

· 4 OUNCES (120 ML) GRILLED PINEAPPLE JUICE (SEE INSTRUCTIONS BELOW)

· 2 OUNCES (60 ML) CANNA-COCONUT CREAM (SEE PAGE 41)

· 1/2 (15 ML) OUNCE DARK RUM

· 1 OUNCE (30 ML) LIGHT RUM

· 1 OUNCE (30 ML) ORGEAT SYRUP

· CRUSHED ICE OR CRUSHED COCONUT WATER ICE, AND ICE CUBES

· GRILLED PINEAPPLE AND GREENISH COCKTAIL CHERRY (SEE PAGE XX), FOR GARNISH

To make the grilled pineapple juice: Remove the core from a fresh pineapple, then slice into 2-inch (5 cm) rounds. Grill on a cast-iron pan or over charcoal for at least 5 minutes per side to help the pineapple caramelize. Let cool, then juice the grilled pineapple following the instructions on your juicer.

Fill a tall Collins glass with crushed ice, then fill a Boston shaker three-quarters full with ice cubes. To the shaker, add the coconut cream, dark rum, light rum, grilled pineapple juice, and orgeat syrup. Shake well, then strain over the ice in the Collins glass, and garnish with a grilled pineapple chunk and a Greenish Cocktail Cherry.

# New Orleans—Style Milk Punch

Intended to help ease the aftereffects of a rough night, the traditional recipe for New Orleans Milk Punch calls for brandy, but I like to make mine with cannabis-infused bourbon instead. When you're choosing a strain to infuse into your bourbon, consider the Veganic Lebanese Love Bomb. (Yes, that's the strain's real name.) This lightly flavored Indica strain displays whiffs of sandalwood on the nose, and it complements the milk punch's creamy texture. And what's more, it practically redefines the word "restorative," so try it in the late morning or early afternoon—or whenever you need a bit of a pick-me-up. You'll notice that this cocktail is light on the bourbon, but don't take this as an invitation to have two in a row: wait for at least an hour before you make a second batch.

## INGREDIENTS

- 1 OUNCE (30 ML) BARRELL BOURBON

- 2 OUNCES (60 ML) CANNABIS CREAM (SEE PAGE 39), MADE WITH HEAVY CREAM

- 2 OUNCES (60 ML) WHOLE MILK

- 1 OUNCE (30 ML) NON-MEDICATED SIMPLE SYRUP

- COUPLE DROPS OF VANILLA EXTRACT

- DASH OF FRESHLY SCRAPED NUTMEG

- CRUSHED ICE

- REGULAR OR CANNABIS-INFUSED COCKTAIL BITTERS

Add all the ingredients except the bitters into a Boston shaker filled three-quarters full with ice cubes. Shake well for 30 seconds. Pour into a coupe glass over crushed ice. Dot with the bitters, and serve immediately.

# To P.G. Hammerton's Delight

This is a cannabis-inflected riff on one of my own recipes—the Cocktail Whisperer's Twisted Frozen Hot Chocolate. To P.G. Hammerton's Delight starts off with a batch of cannabis-infused hot chocolate that's heated low and slow on your stove top. Then it's frozen overnight, before being topped with a dose of navy-strength rum (that is, a rum that clocks in somewhere north of 100 proof) and a spoonful or two of whipped cream. Infuse your heavy cream (and your whipped cream, too, if you like) with the Thin Mint Cookie cannabis strain. It has all the stuffing of the original sweet, earthy Girl Scout Cookie strain, but sports more acidity and a sweet berry taste—and its baked-cookie scents so go well with your carefully-made hot chocolate.

## INGREDIENTS

- 8 OUNCES (225 G) DARK CHOCOLATE
- SUGAR
- 1 PINT (475 ML) CANNABIS-INFUSED HEAVY WHIPPING CREAM (SEE PAGE 39)
- 6 OUNCES (180 ML) HOMEMADE HOT CHOCOLATE

- 1 TEASPOON LECITHIN
- 1 OUNCE (30 ML) HIGH-PROOF RUM
- FRESHLY WHIPPED CREAM, TO SERVE
- EXTRA 1/2 OUNCE (15 ML) RUM, TO SERVE

To make the hot chocolate, melt the dark chocolate in a double boiler with sugar to taste. Add the infused whipping cream. Blend the hot chocolate mixture gently, and heat just below a simmer for 1 hour. Let cool, and stir in the lecithin and rum. Transfer to an airtight container and freeze overnight.

Remove the hot chocolate from the freezer and let sit for a few minutes to "ripen." Scoop into tall glasses, sweeten to taste, if desired, and top with a dollop of infused whipped cream, if you like. Optionally, float an extra 1/4 ounce of rum on top of the whipped cream, and serve immediately.

SERVES 2

# The Golden Leaf Strut

Named for an exceptionally catchy jazz song by the New Orleans Rhythm Kings that had its heyday in the 1920s, the "Golden Leaf Strut" is certain to perk up those flagging taste buds. Tea and citrus are a natural match, and this tall drink combines cooled, strong black tea with a hit of my homemade Lemon-Lime Canna-Shrub for a cocktail that's essential refreshment on a hot summer's day. And, in case you're interested in the lesser-known history of this drink's namesake, the Golden Leaf Strut was a euphemism for smoking cannabis back in the day. Keep the jive going, and make your shrub with the Grandaddy Purple Indica strain. Packed with flavors of lavender and violets, it's sweet in the finish, spicy in the nose, and it marries so well with the tangy, citrus-driven aromatics in the shrub.

## INGREDIENTS

· ICE SPEAR

· 4 OUNCES (120 ML) STRONG ENGLISH BREAKFAST TEA, BREWED, COOLED, AND CHILLED

· 1 OUNCE (30 ML) LEMON-LIME CANNA-SHRUB (SEE PAGE 45)

· RAW HONEY, TO TASTE

Place the ice spear in a Collins glass. Top with the chilled tea, then spoon in the Lemon-Lime Canna-Shrub. Sweeten to taste with raw honey, and serve immediately.

# *If It Keeps on Rainin', Levee's Goin' to Break*

There's no caffeine (or extra sugar, either) in this sneaky little drink, but it's sure to wake up your taste buds—fast. If It Keeps On Rainin' is stepbrother to the mimosa and the Bellini, but you won't find any orange or peach here. Instead, you'll get a blast of bracing tangerine in the form of Fruitations Tangerine craft soda and cocktail mixer. Shake it up with a little melted Canna-Coconut Oil, top it with a splash or two of a bright Spanish cava, and sip it alongside your eggs Benedict or your pancakes with bacon. Use a Sativa strain such as Tangerine to promote wakefulness and clarity: Tangerine's fragrance is a cross between citrus, juicy mango, and caramelized pineapple, and it's a flawless match for both the citrusy mixer and the dry sparkling wine.

## INGREDIENTS

- 1 OUNCE (30 ML) CANNA-COCONUT OIL (SEE PAGE 41)
- 1 OUNCE (30 ML) FRUITATIONS TANGERINE MIXER
- 1 TEASPOON VEGETARIAN LIQUID LECITHIN
- 2 OUNCES (60 ML) DRY SPARKLING WINE, SUCH AS A SPANISH CAVA
- LEMON ZEST TWIST AND CUCUMBER SPEAR, FOR GARNISH

Heat the Canna-Coconut Oil for about 15 seconds in the top of a double boiler, until it turns clear. Then remove it from the heat.

Fill a Boston shaker three-quarters full with ice. Add the liquefied Canna-Coconut Oil, the Fruitations mixer, and the lecithin. Cap and shake hard for 30 seconds. Strain into a champagne flute, and top with the cava. Garnish with the lemon zest twist and the cucumber spear.

CHAPTER

# 05

## BITTERS AND TONICS
### *Revitalizing Cannabis-Infused Cocktails and Mocktails*

I've always been far more interested in classic cocktails than in the trendy, sweet potions that feature in lots of bars and lounges. There's nothing like an Old-Fashioned, brimming with the pungent flavors of rye whiskey and muddled citrus fruit—or a perfectly made Manhattan, in which I can experiment with different kinds of vermouth. And what about the crisp simplicity of a gin and tonic? Time-honored potables like these offer endless ways for intrepid bartenders to rework and re-create them. And that's exactly what this chapter aims to do.

Of course, the drinks in this chapter do contain a common ingredient: cannabis. There are lots of different ways to work cannabis into cocktails and mocktails—but remember that each cannabis strain is unique, and will produce different physical and mental effects. Again, Indicas tend to help you kick back and relax, while Sativas heighten concentration levels and make you feel more alert or uplifted.

CANNABIS COCKTAILS, MOCKTAILS, AND TONICS

While I recommend specific strains to complement the ingredients in each drink, you should always ask your caregiver for advice on which strains are right for you, depending on your personal needs and your medical history. Do keep an eye on your body's reactions to cannabis and cannabis cocktails as you enjoy these classic drinks: you may not react to cannabis in the same way that, say, your brother or your best friend does. And I can't say it often enough: Go slow when you're imbibing. Clear your schedule for the evening, if you must. Have one cocktail or mocktail per hour at most, and don't pick up your car keys for at least 12 hours after you've finished drinking.

Cannabis is just one of the ingredients in these cocktails, though, and it's not the only one that's reputed to have healing properties. Historically, the vermouth in the Mezzrole Cocktail and the Dramatis Personae contained a veritable laundry list of beneficial herbs that could be used to treat scads of illnesses and afflictions. And if you can't imagine combining vermouth with cannabis, consider these two facts: early apothecaries used vermouth as a hair tonic to treat head lice. Certain strains of cannabis are insect repellents. Could there be a connection? I'll leave the conclusions up to you.

Then there's root tea liqueur, which turns up in my Thai-Spiced Ginger Beer. Back in the eighteenth century, colonial settlers learned how to make this potent tonic from Native Americans. Made with local roots, herbs, and barks, it was the granddaddy of root beer, which was first produced during the years of Temperance—though, of course, far more powerful than the original. These days, a few craft distillers have revived the traditional root tea recipe, and it's worth getting your hands on a bottle for the history alone.

And by now, you're already well acquainted with the curative qualities inherent in bitters, which pepper lots of the cocktails in this book. Hangovers, dyspepsia, general nausea—all of these would have been treated with a dash of aromatic bitters in days gone by. Try bitters by The Bitter End (bitterendbitters.com). They're a top-class small producer: all their bitters are made by hand, and they use all-natural ingredients.

Here's to healing what ails you!

# The Mezzrole Cocktail

I'm a huge fan of Manhattan-style cocktails; they make great aperitifs. This one is named after Milton "Mezz" Mezzrow, a jazz musician who lived in Harlem in the 1920s. And, as Mezz himself would have known, the term for a well-rolled cannabis cigarette was a "mezzrole"—so I just had to commemorate both man and medicine in this elegant cocktail. It combines cannabis-infused sweet vermouth, handmade cocktail cherries, and quality bourbon into a small, but well-formed, libation that's deeply healing. When you're infusing your vermouth, consider choosing a Sativa-Indica hybrid strain called Cherry Pie. It's redolent of sweet and sour cherries, and it complements the toasty, oaky flavors inherent in the liquors. As for making crushed ice, it's best to place the ice in a Lewis bag—a heavy canvas bag that's made for the job—before whacking it with a wooden mallet or rolling pin.

## INGREDIENTS

- 4-6 GREENISH COCKTAIL CHERRIES (SEE PAGE 45)
- 1/2 OUNCE (15 ML) CANNABIS-INFUSED VERMOUTH, SUCH AS UNCOUTH VERMOUTH'S SEASONAL WILDFLOWER BLEND
- HANDFUL OF CRUSHED ICE
- 1 OUNCE (30 ML) BOURBON WHISKEY
- AROMATIC BITTERS

Muddle the Greenish Cocktail Cherries with a wooden muddler or the handle of a wooden spoon, then top with the vermouth. Continue to muddle for 30 seconds to combine the flavors. Cover with the crushed ice. Top with the bourbon, then dot with aromatic bitters. Don't have two: one should be more than enough.

# Up the Lazy River

As any gin connoisseur will tell you, quality gin made the traditional way is a beautiful thing on its own. But Vermont-based distillers Barr Hill are taking things one step further: they're making gin that's been infused with antioxidant-rich raw honey. And it makes a gin and tonic that's absolutely otherworldly. You don't have to stop there, though. Try infusing a Barr Hill gin with an Indica strain such as Master Kush, which is earthy, pungent, and sweet all at once. It's an ideal match for both the juniper-and-spice flavor of the gin and the lightly-sweetened tonic water. Then, turn your G&T into an Up the Lazy River by adding a splash of lager beer (don't ask: just do it) and a dash of curry bitters (like the ones made by The Bitter End (bitterendbitters.com).

## INGREDIENTS

· 3 ICE CUBES

· 1 OUNCE (30 ML) CANNABIS-INFUSED BARR HILL GIN

· 4 OUNCES (120 ML) CANE SUGAR–BASED TONIC WATER, SUCH AS Q TONIC

· SCANT SPLASH OF LAGER BEER

· 2-3 DROPS CURRY BITTERS FROM THE BITTER END

Fill a Collins glass with the ice. Add the gin, then top with the tonic water and beer. Finish with 2 to 3 drops of the curry bitters. Serve immediately.

# A Fearful Gale

Cannabis doesn't come cheap, so when you're making tinctures and infusions, you'll want to honor it by pairing it with the best-quality spirits you can afford. When I'm making a cannabis-infused rum, I always reach for a bottle of Rhum Agricole, which hails from Martinique in the West Indies. Rhum Agricole is made from fresh sugarcane juice rather than molasses, and it's much better than the mainstream stuff you'll find on the shelves of your local liquor store. Get your hands on some, then try combining it with Pineapple Skunk, a hybrid strain with aromatics of crushed pineapple, freshly turned soil, and baby skunk. (Relax: that's a good thing.) Then, mix your infused rum into a slushy, refreshing Fearful Gale: crushed coconut water ice, covered with Rhum Agricole, plus tonic water, lime juice, and hand-grated nutmeg.

## INGREDIENTS

- CRUSHED COCONUT WATER ICE

- 3 OUNCES (90 ML) CANE SUGAR–BASED TONIC WATER, SUCH AS Q TONIC

- 2 OUNCES (60 ML) CANNABIS-INFUSED RHUM AGRICOLE

- 1 OUNCE (30 ML) FRESHLY SQUEEZED LIME JUICE

- LIME WEDGES

- FRESHLY GRATED NUTMEG

Fill a 16-ounce (475 ml) juice glass three-quarters full with the coconut water ice. Add the tonic water, then float the Rhum Agricole on top. Add the lime juice, stir, and squeeze a lime wedge into the drink. Scrape a little fresh nutmeg over the top, and serve immediately.

# Thai-Spiced Ginger Beer

It's tough to improve on small-batch, cane sugar-based ginger beer, but I've discovered that it's doable. Hence, my Thai-Spiced Ginger Beer, which doctors up quality ginger beer with chilled spearmint tea—great for the digestion—and a portion of organic root liqueur. (Years ago, apothecaries would have prescribed root teas to quiet a colicky child, to treat a fever, or even to relax a contusion caused by a kick from a cow or horse. These days, artisan distillers are turning these teas into delicious liqueurs.) Seal the deal with an ounce of medicated raw honey syrup made with hybrid cannabis strain Tangie. It's crisp, earthy, and gingery, and it's more than a match for the unusual aromatics in the root tea liqueur.

## INGREDIENTS

- LEMON ZEST ICE (SIMPLY FREEZE FRESHLY GRATED LEMON ZEST INTO HOMEMADE ICE CUBES)
- 1 BOTTLE (6 OUNCES, OR 175 ML) OF CANE SUGAR–BASED, NONALCOHOLIC GINGER BEER
- 1 OUNCE (30 ML) ORGANIC ROOT TEA LIQUEUR

- 2 OUNCES (60 ML) SPEARMINT TEA, BREWED, THEN COOLED
- 1 OUNCE (15 ML) MEDICATED RICH SIMPLE SYRUP (SEE PAGE 43), MADE WITH RAW HONEY
- 2 DROPS JAMAICAN JERK BITTERS FROM THE BITTER END
- CANNABIS FLOWER OR SPRIG OF THAI BASIL, FOR GARNISH

Fill a Collins glass with the lemon zest ice cubes. Pour in the ginger beer, then add the root tea liqueur. Add the iced spearmint tea, then the Medicated Rich Simple Syrup. Stir gently. Finish with two drops of the jerk bitters. Garnish with either a cannabis flower or a sprig of Thai basil. Serve with a couple long straws. Sip slowly, and wait at least an hour before you pour yourself another.

# Dramatis Personae

The Dramatis Personae is my Cocktail Whisperer's riff on the Vieux Carré, the classic New Orleans cocktail. My version calls for belly-friendly Creole bitters, and uses calvados, or apple brandy, in place of cognac. Sound like an unusual cast of characters? It gets better. Enter a spritz of Infused Absinthe, stage right: Finish the Dramatis Personae by pouring a little Infused Absinthe into an atomizer or spray bottle, and topping the drink with just a whiff of the medicated spirit. When you're infusing your absinthe, try an Indica strain like Mr. Nice. It's earthy and sweet, with pungent aromatics that enhance the aniseed and herbal notes in the absinthe.

## INGREDIENTS

- MARIJUANA SMOKE, TO FLAVOR THE MIXING GLASS
- ICE
- 1/2 OUNCE (15 ML) RYE WHISKEY
- 1/2 OUNCE (15 ML) SWEET VERMOUTH
- 1/4 OUNCE CALVADOS
- 3-4 SHAKES CREOLE-STYLE BITTERS
- 2-3 SHAKES AROMATIC BITTERS
- SPRITZ OF INFUSED ABSINTHE (SEE PAGE 38)

Before you fill your mixing glass with ice, turn it upside down and burn some cannabis under it in order to fill it with smoke. Turn it right side up, and immediately fill it three-quarters full with ice. (Now you've made smoked ice!) Add all the other ingredients except the absinthe, and stir fifty times. Strain into a prechilled glass, and finish with a spritz of Infused Absinthe.

# This Was the Day of Incidents

As nineteenth- and early twentieth-century sailors would have known first-hand, being at sea is no pleasure trip—unless your idea of fun is fighting pouring rain, crashing waves, and gale-force winds just to keep your vessel afloat. The only thing to do would have been to listen carefully to your captain's orders, and to look forward to the portion of rum and hot tea that—hopefully—awaited you at the end of your long workday. If you're suffering the effects of a day of incidents like this one, whip up a Day of Incidents to combat the pain. You'll add cannabis-infused cane syrup to chilled, strong black tea and dark rum. Make yours with a Sativa strain such as Columbian Gold, with its pungent signature aromatics of baby skunk, freshly cut thyme and lavender, and crushed pine needles, showcased against the backdrop of the tannic black tea.

## INGREDIENTS

· COCONUT WATER ICE CUBES

· 6 OUNCES (180 ML) STRONG BLACK TEA, BREWED THEN COOLED

· 2 OUNCES (60 ML) STORE-BOUGHT CANE SUGAR SYRUP, COMBINED WITH NO MORE THAN 10 ML CANNABIS TINCTURE OF YOUR CHOICE

· 1 OUNCE (30 ML) HIGH-PROOF DARK RUM

· AROMATIC BITTERS

· FRESHLY GRATED NUTMEG

Fill a tall plastic cup with coconut water ice cubes. Add the tea, the medicated cane sugar syrup, and rum. Mix gently. Dot with bitters, and scrape a little fresh nutmeg over the top. Perfect for thirsty armchair sailors.

# The Peeler

The Moscow mule is traditionally made with vodka and ginger beer—but I think this rum-driven version is so much better. In the Peeler, a portion of dark rum is flanked by fresh citrus juices (no scurvy on board, please) and a measure of medicated ginger syrup. Ginger syrup is a powerful remedy for nausea and seasickness, as every nineteenth-century ship's doctor would have known, and so is cannabis: together, they're even more effective. Infuse your Medicated Rich Ginger Simple Syrup with Berry White, a gorgeous hybrid strain that sings of freshly crushed red and blue fruits, and harmonizes perfectly with the citrus juices and the dark rum.

## INGREDIENTS

- 2 HANDFULS CRUSHED COCONUT WATER ICE

- 2 OUNCES (60 ML) MEDICATED RICH GINGER SIMPLE SYRUP (SEE PAGE 43)

- 1 OUNCE (30 ML) NON-MEDICATED COCONUT CREAM

- 1 OUNCE (30 ML) FRESHLY SQUEEZED LIME JUICE

- 1/2 OUNCE (15 ML) FRESHLY SQUEEZED ORANGE JUICE

- 1 OUNCE (30 ML) DARK RUM

- 4 OUNCES (120 ML) SELTZER WATER

- AROMATIC BITTERS

Add the crushed ice, Medicated Rich Ginger Simple Syrup, coconut cream, citrus juices, and rum to a blender. Blend for a few seconds until combined. Pour into a Collins glass. Top with the seltzer, then dot with aromatic bitters. The result is a liquid vacation to the islands.

# The John Knox Preface

Mocktails that pair infused syrups with freshly squeezed juices are so good that you won't notice—or care—that they're alcohol-free. The key is to stick to freshly squeezed juices. I never use anything that comes out of a bottle, and early pharmacists wouldn't have, either: fruits and fruit juices would have had to be consumed immediately or woven into a vinegar-based shrub for later use. This sumptuous punch is spiked with a medicated, raw honey simple syrup that's best made with an Indica strain such as Pure Kush. Then it's topped with a bottle of bubbles: use seltzer water or—if you don't mind adding alcohol to the mix—a bottle or two of chilled Cava.

## INGREDIENTS

- 1/2 QUART (475 ML) GRILLED PINEAPPLE JUICE

- 1 QUART (950 ML) FRESHLY SQUEEZED ORANGE JUICE

- 1/2 QUART (475 ML) FRESHLY SQUEEZED LEMON JUICE

- 1 QUART (950 ML) POMEGRANATE JUICE

- 1/2 QUART (475 ML) CRANBERRY JUICE

- 2 CUPS (475 ML) MEDICATED RICH SIMPLE SYRUP (SEE PAGE 43), MADE WITH RAW HONEY

- 20 DROPS MOROCCAN BITTERS FROM THE BITTER END, OR MORE TO TASTE

- 1 LITER SELTZER WATER, OR 1-2 BOTTLES (750 ML) OF CHILLED CAVA

- COCONUT WATER ICE CUBES

To make the grilled pineapple juice: Remove the core from 4 fresh pineapples, then slice into 2-inch (5 cm) rounds. Grill in batches on a cast-iron pan or over charcoal for at least 5 minutes per side to help the pineapple caramelize. Let cool, then juice the grilled pineapple following the instructions on your juicer.

Mix all the juices and the simple syrup together in a large punch bowl. Top with the Moroccan bitters. Add the Cava and mix gently. Place an ice cube in each of 10 teacups. Top with the punch, and serve to your guests immediately.

SERVES 10 OR MORE

# Aw, Boys! Y'all Didn't Have To Do This

Belgian beer has always been like mother's milk to me. Growing up, I loved learning about the Trappist monks' rich history of folk healing—and as I got older, I became equally excited by their beers. *Kriek*, a style of lambic beer, can be either sweet or dry. It's made by fermenting lambic with sour cherries and their pits, and it's often aged inside ancient wooden casks. Try adding a few drops of your favorite cannabis infusion to it: I think the Indica strain Black Romulan is a great match for Kriek, with its aromatics of crushed pine needles. Just remember to stick to 10 milliliters of your favorite infusion, or even less. No sense in becoming out of sorts, after all.

## INGREDIENTS

· 1 BOTTLE (375 ML) OF CHILLED KRIEK, DRY OR SWEET

· CANNABIS INFUSION OF YOUR CHOICE: NO MORE THAN 10 ML

Carefully pour the Kriek beer into a Belgian beer glass. Add the cannabis infusion, and mix gently with a long-handled spoon. Serve immediately.

# Cocktail Whisperer's Painkilling System #2016

**Grilled fruit juice is one of my secret weapons. As the fruit caramelizes, its flavors become sweeter and more nuanced. Pineapples, for instance, benefit big-time from a few minutes on the grill—or, if it's doable, a wood fire! So, don't be tempted to skip this step when you're making my Painkilling System #2016. Make your infusion with the best rum you can get your mitts on, such as Jersey Artisan Distilling's Busted Barrel rum. Pair it with Afgoo, a powerful Indica strain that's sweet, spicy, oh-so-relaxing, and a gorgeous match for the toasty, burnt-sugar flavors of the grilled fruit juice.**

## INGREDIENTS

- 4 OUNCES (120 ML) GRILLED PINEAPPLE JUICE (SEE INSTRUCTIONS BELOW)

- 1¼ OUNCES (45 ML) CANNABIS-INFUSED DARK RUM

- 1 OUNCE (30 ML) ORGEAT SYRUP

- 2 OUNCES (60 ML) NON-MEDICATED COCONUT CREAM

- 2 OUNCES (60 ML) FRESHLY SQUEEZED BLOOD ORANGE JUICE

- AROMATIC BITTERS

- ICE

To make the grilled pineapple juice: Remove the core from a fresh pineapple, then slice into 2-inch (5 cm) rounds. Grill on a cast-iron pan or over charcoal for at least 5 minutes per side to help the pineapple caramelize. Let cool, then juice the grilled pineapple following the instructions on your juicer.

Fill a Boston shaker three-quarters full with ice and add all the ingredients except the bitters, reserving 1/2 ounce (15 ml) of the rum to float on top of the finished drinks. Shake hard, then pour into two coupe glasses. Float 1/4 ounce rum on top of each drink. Dot with the aromatic bitters, and watch your pain sail away.

SERVES 2

# 06

## AFTERNOON LIVENERS
### *Potable Pick-Me-Ups with Gut-Healing Shrubs and Mood-Enhancing Syrups*

We've all suffered through bouts of the dreaded mid-afternoon slump. You know how it goes: your morning coffee's long since worn off; you're still kind of stuffed from the enchiladas you had for lunch; and the day's end shimmers in the distance like a far-off oasis.

Well, traveler, you might be in need of a little liquid refreshment. Don't pour yourself a second coffee. You don't want a rush of jittery nerves, anyway, and too much coffee can screw up your sleep patterns, even if you finish your last *caffé* long before you head to bed. Instead, turn to the drinks in this chapter to revive flagging spirits, boost energy levels, and calm a queasy belly. They're made with a number of ingredients that have been used for centuries to address afflictions like these—such as homemade shrubs, absinthe, and fresh citrus juices.

I'm a major advocate of gut-healing shrubs. They were the original energy drink—long before those sugar-laden alternatives hit the market—and they've got a venerable Middle Eastern pedigree. Their name derives from the Middle Eastern term *sharb*, which simply means "a drink." Over the years, a "shrub" came to refer to an acidulated, sweetened fruit syrup that could be added to water or enjoyed over crushed ice as a warm-weather treat. And, of course, thanks to the fact that they're made with vinegar, they were also a way to preserve seasonal fruits, vegetables, and herbs for longer-term use—a technique early apothecaries used to make the most of the bounty of their kitchen gardens.

These days, shrubs can still pep up lackluster appetites, or provide tender care for stomachs suffering the consequences of an excess of good food and drink. They also make great additions to cocktails and mocktails. You can also simply add the shrub to some soda water for a non-medicated quaff. But if you don't want to go to the trouble of making your own shrub, that's okay: use a store-bought version instead. (I won't tell anyone.)

Absinthe, too, turns up in lots of the cocktails in this chapter. That's partly because it's an effective digestif—but it's also because absinthe tends to make the drinker feel alert and awake,

rather than relaxed and sleepy. It was first used as a medicinal tonic in eighteenth-century France, and some contemporary versions such as Jade Liqueurs' Esprit Edouard absinthe are remarkable for their authenticity: they have the power to transport me back in time to nineteenth-century Paris with a single sip. Try a cannabis-infused absinthe in cocktails like the icy Hoodoo Man on page 98, my rendition of the classic New Orleans absinthe frappe, especially during the dog days of summer.

And fresh citrus juices, with their palate-lifting acidity, are vital in this chapter. They're bursting with vitamin C, and they're a surprisingly good match for both quality spirits and cannabis—or, if you're so inclined, just one and not the other. My Mock-Cosmopolitan, for instance, relies on fresh citrus for its refreshing, party-time flavor, and it's best made with a cannabis-infused simple syrup: it's alcohol-free, but it's got so much kick that you'd never know it.

At the risk of sounding like a broken record: Don't rush when you're sipping the enlivening drinks in this chapter. Stick to a single drink per hour. Then enjoy it meditatively and peacefully, and let the day unfold.

# 608 Bush Street

There's simply no substitute for real maple syrup. Try it once—over a stack of piping hot pancakes, in a vinaigrette, or in a cocktail—and it'll linger in your memory forever. So throw out that cheap butter-flavored corn-syrup substitute; invest in a bottle of the bona fide stuff. Then, use it in place of the traditional sugar cube in my 608 Bush Street, a twisted version of the classic Sazerac cocktail. For your absinthe wash, use an absinthe you've infused with Sour OG, a hybrid strain with notes of pine, lemon, and the minerally scent of wet gravel. It's just the right counterpoint to the aromatics of the absinthe, and it's essential to this finely balanced drink.

## INGREDIENTS

- 1/2 OUNCE (15 ML) INFUSED ABSINTHE (SEE PAGE 38)
- 1/2 OUNCE (15 ML) DARK MAPLE SYRUP
- 1/2 OUNCE (15 ML) WHITE BALSAMIC VINEGAR
- 1/4 OUNCE CALVADOS
- 1/4 OUNCE RYE WHISKEY
- 3 SHAKES CREOLE-STYLE BITTERS
- LEMON PEEL TWIST, FOR GARNISH
- CRUSHED ICE

Wash a chilled old-fashioned glass with the absinthe by pouring it into the glass, swirling it around, and pouring it out (into your mouth, if you like!). Fill the glass half full with crushed ice, set aside to chill for a few minutes, then discard the ice.

Fill a mixing glass three-quarters full with ice. Add the maple syrup, vinegar, calvados, and whiskey. Mix gently. Add the Creole-style bitters, and mix again. Strain over the crushed ice into the glass, and garnish with a lemon peel twist. Oh my . . .

# The Ancient Healer Cocktail (Ti-Punch-esque)

**Influenced by "ti' punch," the old-fashioned sailor's pick-me-up, the Ancient Healer is an exercise in minimalism. But there's no better restorative after a long day.**

━━━━━━━━━━━━━━━ INGREDIENTS ━━━━━━━━━━━━━━━

### For the Ginger-Lime Shrub:

- PEELED ZEST OF 4 WELL-WASHED LIMES (discard the pith: it's very bitter)
- 4 LIMES (ABOVE), QUARTERED
- 1 CUP (200 G) DEMERARA SUGAR
- 6 TABLESPOONS (48 G) FRESHLY GRATED GINGERROOT
- 1-2 CUPS (235 TO 475 ML) APPLE CIDER VINEGAR (depending on the height of the ingredients when placed in a bowl)

### For the Ancient Healer cocktail:

- 2-3 CHUNKS LIME, SKIN ON
- 2 TABLESPOONS (30 ML) GINGER-LIME SHRUB (SEE DIRECTIONS BELOW)
- 1 OUNCE (30 ML) CANNABIS-INFUSED, 100-PROOF RHUM AGRICOLE
- 1 OUNCE (30 ML) STORE-BOUGHT CANE SUGAR SYRUP

First, make the shrub. In a nonreactive bowl, combine the sugar, zest, lime chunks, and ginger. Stir and coat all the fruit with sugar. Cover and leave at room temperature at least overnight or for 1 to 2 days. Now prepare your shrub for aging. Set a strainer over another nonreactive bowl, and pour the lime chunks and ginger into the strainer. Use a stout wooden spoon to extract as much juice as possible. Let the mixture sit for a few more hours. Stir again, and discard the fruit chunks. Stir in the vinegar, then use a funnel to transfer the shrub syrup to a sterilized bottle. Seal, and shake well. Store the bottles in the frige or cellar for 3 to 4 weeks before using. Shake each bottle once or twice daily to help dissolve the sugar. When it's mostly dissolved, your shrub is ready. Makes 1½ cups. Keep refrigerated, and use within 6 months.

Then, make the cocktail. Place the lime chunks into a small cut-crystal glass. Add the Ginger-Lime Shrub, then the Rhum Agricole and the cane sugar syrup. Muddle together using a muddler or the end of a small wooden spoon. Serve immediately.

# The Albion K. Parris Double Old–Fashioned

The Old-Fashioned has often been imitated, but it's rarely been improved—
until now, that is. Enter the Albion K. Parris Double Old-Fashioned, in which
caramelized oranges are muddled with a homemade medicated cocktail
cherry and a sugar cube drenched in orange bitters. Topped with a full
two ounces of rye whiskey—hence the "double" old-fashioned—and a dash
of seltzer, the Albion K. is not for the faint of heart. (Consider yourself
warned.) Infuse your whiskey with an XXX OG strain; it's an Indica, and its
flavors of roasted coffee, crushed citrus, and newly turned soil are just
what cinnamony rye whiskey needs. Oh, and in case you're curious, the
fabulously named Albion K. Parris was the mayor of Portland, Maine in 1852.
Now you know.

---

### INGREDIENTS

- 1 SUGAR CUBE

- SEVERAL DROPS OF ORANGE BITTERS

- 3 GRILLED ORANGE SLICES

- 1 GREENISH COCKTAIL CHERRY
  (SEE PAGE 45)

- 2 OUNCES (60 ML) CANNABIS-
  INFUSED RYE WHISKEY
  (MINIMUM 100 PROOF)

- SPLASH OF SODA WATER

. . . . . . . . . . . . . . . . . . . . . . . . . . . . . . . . . . . . . . . . . . . . . . . . . . .

To grill orange slices: Peel and thickly slice 1 orange. Place 3 slices on a hot
cast-iron pan (or over charcoal) for 3 minutes per side to help the fruit caramelize.
Let cool.

Place the sugar cube in an old-fashioned glass, and soak with several drops of
orange bitters. Add the grilled orange segments and the Greenish Cocktail Cherry,
and muddle well with a muddler or the end of a wooden spoon. Add the infused
whiskey, and muddle again to mix. Top with a splash of seltzer water, then serve
immediately.

# Candy Says

Down in the West Indies, the restaurants on the island of St. Barthelemy—St. Barth's for short—are famous for their many versions of rum punch. Don't be fooled, though; these rum punches bear zero resemblance to the sickly sweet red stuff served in plastic cups at college frat parties. The recipes for these punches date back to the eighteenth century (if not earlier), and they're as authentic as it gets. Made with Rhum Agricole, Candy Says takes its inspiration from these recipes—with, of course, the addition of a cannabis-infused simple syrup. I suggest making yours with the hybrid strain Key Lime Pie: it's a great match for rum and fresh fruit juices, thanks to its aromatics of cotton candy, citrus, bittersweet chocolate, and exotic Caribbean spices.

## INGREDIENTS

- COCONUT WATER ICE

- 2 OUNCES (60 ML) 100-PROOF RHUM AGRICOLE

- 1 OUNCE (30 ML) NON-MEDICATED COCONUT CREAM

- 2 OUNCES (60 ML) FRESHLY SQUEEZED ORANGE JUICE

- 1 HANDFUL FRESH RASPBERRIES, CRUSHED WITH A WOODEN SPOON

- 1 TEASPOON GROUND TURMERIC

- 2 OUNCES (60 ML) MEDICATED RICH SIMPLE SYRUP (SEE PAGE 43), MADE WITH RAW HONEY

- 2 OUNCES (60 ML) CANE SYRUP–BASED GINGER BEER

- 6 DROPS AROMATIC BITTERS

Fill a Boston shaker half full with the coconut water ice. Add the Rhum Agricole, coconut cream, orange juice, raspberries, turmeric, and Medicated Rich Simple Syrup, and shake hard for about 15 seconds. Divide between two miniature coupe glasses. Top each with 1 ounce (30 ml) of ginger beer, and dot with the aromatic bitters to finish.

SERVES 2

# At Last a Paltry Decree

~~~~~~~~~~~~~~~~~~~~~~~~~~~~~~~~~~~~~~~~~~~~~~~~~~~~~~~~~~~~~~

While it's true that freshly squeezed juices are always the best way to honor your fine spirits (and your cannabis), things—spills, spoilage—happen. That's when you'll be glad you had a top-quality mixer on hand to save the day. Try Fruitations tangerine craft soda and cocktail mixer (justaddfruitations.com) in this lightly-sparkling, citrusy cocktail. (Fruitations mixers are always handcrafted and only use three ingredients: fruit, water, and cane sugar.) But first, add a little medicine to your mixer: that is, a cannabis tincture of your choice. Consider making your tincture with the Sativa-hybrid strain Gelato, which has the spicy fruitiness of homemade sherbet, plus the crushed-cookie scent that's indigenous to the Girl Scout Cookies strain. Its natural sweetness brings out the best in the rum and absinthe—and in the tangerine syrup, too.

## INGREDIENTS

- 1 OUNCE (30 ML) 100-PROOF RHUM AGRICOLE

- 1/10 OUNCE ABSINTHE, SUCH AS JADE LIQUEURS' ESPRIT EDOUARD ABSINTHE

- 2 OUNCES (60 ML) FRUITATIONS TANGERINE MIXER, COMBINED WITH NO MORE THAN 10 ML CANNABIS TINCTURE OF YOUR CHOICE

- 2 OUNCES (60 ML) SPARKLING WATER

- 2-4 DASHES LEMON BITTERS

- GRAPEFRUIT ZEST TWIST, FOR GARNISH

- 1 GLÄCE LUXURY ICE G-CUBED

Fill a Boston shaker three-quarters full with ice. Add the Rhum Agricole, absinthe, and cannabis-infused mixer. Shake hard for ten seconds. Place an ice cube into an old-fashioned glass, then strain the mixture over it. Top with a splash of sparkling water, then dot with the bitters, and garnish with the grapefruit zest twist. Serve!

# John Bartram's Garden Punch

You may have tried a garden-variety garden punch before, but I guarantee you've never had anything like this unorthodox take on the classic mid-afternoon refresher. Named after the self-taught, eighteenth-century American botanist, this herbed garden punch is made with gin, fresh grapefruit juice, and a bouquet of fragrant herbs—and it's spiked with a cannabis-infused simple syrup that's best made with a Sativa strain such as Exodus. With its scents of *fraise de bois* (that is, tiny, intensely-flavored strawberries) and crushed stones, Exodus works beautifully with the botanicals in gin—and those gravelly, crushed-stone aromatics act as the bedrock that underlies and connects the punch's flavors. Choose a very, very dry sparkling rosé here; you'll want to add color and flavor, not extra sugar.

## INGREDIENTS

- 1 CUP (WEIGHT WILL VARY) ASSORTED FRESHLY SNIPPED HERBS, SUCH AS THYME, ROSEMARY, SAGE, AND FENNEL FRONDS

- 1 CUP (235 ML) MEDICATED RICH SIMPLE SYRUP (SEE PAGE 43)

- 2 QUARTS (1.9 L) FRESHLY SQUEEZED PINK GRAPEFRUIT JUICE

- 1 BOTTLE (750 ML) OF GIN

- 2 BOTTLES (1500 ML TOTAL) OF DRY SPARKLING ROSÉ WINE

- 20 SHAKES OF AROMATIC BITTERS

- 1 GLÄCE LUXURY ICE MARIKO SPHERE

Mix the herbs in a fine-mesh hemp or nylon bag, and tie closed with kitchen string. Add the Medicated Rich Simple Syrup, grapefruit juice, and gin to a large punch bowl, and stir gently to combine. Submerge the bag of herbs in the mixture, cover the bowl with plastic wrap, and store in the refrigerator overnight. Before serving, remove the bag from the punch and discard the contents. Add the sparkling wine and the aromatic bitters, and stir gently again to combine. Serve immediately.

SERVES 10 OR MORE

# *Pour calmer le moi intérieur*

When you're using top-quality spirits, you don't need to add bells and whistles to make great cocktails, and the Pour calmer le moi intérieur—"to calm my interior" in French—is liquid proof. Get ahold of a bottle of Jade Liqueurs' Esprit Edouard absinthe, an authentic, contemporary re-creation of the notorious nineteenth-century tipple. It's delicious without the addition of cannabis, but if you choose to infuse, go for the invigorating Sativa strain Sour Diesel. With its open-can-of-diesel-fuel nose and spicy, citrus-driven finish, it's magnificent with the smoky, mysterious aniseed notes in the absinthe. And the absinthe really is the star of the show here; all it needs for backup is a little cool spring water, and a dot or two of aromatic bitters. Stick to the less-is-more rule and have just one of these elegant cocktails; the idea is to calm, enlighten, and refresh.

## INGREDIENTS

- 1 OUNCE (30 ML) INFUSED ABSINTHE (SEE PAGE 38)
- 4 OUNCES (120 ML) COOL SPRING WATER
- 2-3 DROPS AROMATIC BITTERS

Add the Infused Absinthe to an old-fashioned glass. Slowly add the water, then stir gently. Dot with the aromatic bitters. Sip slowly and thoughtfully.

# *Medicated Smoky Roy*

As a kid, I remember watching my grandfather enjoying Rob Roy cocktails made with the blended Scotch whiskey from the bottle with the white label. Since then, I've always thought of it as "his" drink, although I never asked him why he liked it so much. Perhaps it was a matter of contrasts—the way the peat-smoke flavor of the whiskey shines through the sticky-sweet vermouth. I'll never know for sure, but what's certain is that the Rob Roy is my own liquid connection to my late grandfather. So this medicated version is dedicated to him. The Rob Roy is the perfect foil for an Indica infusion, which is why you should make your infused Scotch with Indica strain Brand X, which is practically swirling with the smoky, foresty scents of crushed pine needles and spearmint: it harmonizes wonderfully with the vermouth's herbaceous qualities.

## INGREDIENTS

- 1¼ (45 ML) OUNCES CANNABIS-INFUSED SCOTCH WHISKEY

- 1 OUNCE (30 ML) SWEET FRENCH VERMOUTH

- DASH OF AROMATIC BITTERS

- 1 GREENISH COCKTAIL CHERRY (SEE PAGE 45)

- ICE

Fill a martini glass with ice and top with a little water. Set aside for a few minutes to chill, then discard the ice water.

Fill a cocktail mixing glass three-quarters full with ice. Add the whiskey and the vermouth, and stir exactly nineteen times. (Just trust me.) Strain into the prechilled glass and dot with the bitters. Garnish with a Greenish Cocktail Cherry.

# Benny Goodman Fizz

Named for the King of Swing himself, the Benny Goodman Fizz is light on its feet. It's sparkling, refreshing, and sophisticated, and it's best when it's crafted with barrel-aged gin, like Barr Hill's Tom Cat gin. This unique style of gin dates back to the Middle Ages, when juniper—one of gin's essential ingredients—was thought to ward off the plague. (Needless to say, it wasn't terribly effective.) These days, though, barrel-aged gin is more about pleasure than it is about medicine. Aged in new, charred American oak barrels gives Tom Cat a toasty, vanilla-tinged finish perfect for infusing with a Sativa strain like Maui Waui (that's pronounced "wowee," by the way), which boasts flavors of sweet pineapple and a finish that's reminiscent of sea-salt-coated stones. And it takes to the rose syrup and the gin like a kitten to a drippy sprinkler: that is, with boundless enthusiasm and affection.

## INGREDIENTS

- 1 OUNCE (30 ML) CANNABIS-INFUSED GIN
- 2 OUNCES (60 ML) STORE-BOUGHT ROSE SIMPLE SYRUP
- 1 OUNCE (30 ML) SELTZER WATER
- 3-4 DROPS GRAPEFRUIT BITTERS
- JADE LIQUEURS' ESPRIT EDOUARD ABSINTHE IN AN ATOMIZER (MEDICATED, A PLUS!)
- LONG GRAPEFRUIT ZEST TWIST
- ICE

Fill a Collins glass with ice and top with a little water. Set aside for a few minutes to chill, then discard the ice water.

Fill a Boston shaker three-quarters full with ice. Add the gin and the rose simple syrup, then shake hard for 12 seconds. Pour into a coupe glass and add the seltzer water. Dot with the grapefruit bitters, spray the top of the drink with the absinthe, and garnish with a grapefruit zest twist.

# The Hoodoo Man

Ever heard of an absinthe frappe? It's a New Orleans staple, and it was originally made with absinthe, anisette (an anise-flavored liqueur that's popular in France, Italy, and Spain), and soda water. The Hoodoo Man is my Cocktail Whisperer's take on the nineteenth-century tipple. Except mine, of course, has a couple of twists: it involves muddled mint, Jade absinthe, and a dose of cannabis-infused simple syrup. Choose a Sativa strain when you're concocting your simple syrup, such as Jamaican Lion. Herbal, spicy, and sweet, Jamaican Lion pairs well with both the absinthe and the fresh mint. The result is a stimulating drink that's perfect for hot August afternoons. Go especially slowly when you're combining absinthe and cannabis; one of these Hoodoos goes quite a long way.

## INGREDIENTS

- 5-6 FRESH MINT LEAVES

- 1¼ OUNCES (45 ML) NON-MEDICATED JADE LIQUEURS' ESPRIT EDOUARD ABSINTHE

- 4 OUNCES (120 ML) SELTZER WATER

- CRUSHED ICE

- 1/2 OUNCE (15 ML) MEDICATED RICH SIMPLE SYRUP (SEE PAGE 43)

Place the fresh mint leaves in a pint glass. Using a muddler or the end of a wooden spoon, muddle them to release their fragrant natural oils. Add the absinthe and muddle for a few seconds more. Add the seltzer water, then top with the crushed ice, and drizzle with the Medicated Rich Simple Syrup. Serve with two small straws.

# Mock-Cosmopolitan

**My activated mocktail version of the classic Cosmo has all the stuffing of the original. Minus the vodka, of course, and the standard, generally-undrinkable triple sec, which is of dubious origin anyway. Good riddance. Instead, it's topped up with the raw honey version of my Medicated Rich Simple Syrup, which I like to make with Sativa-hybrid strain Super Lemon Haze. It's got notes of crushed citrus fruits woven around a core of tropical spices and light stone fruits, and it really takes to freshly squeezed fruit juices. Before you start pouring yourself seconds, remember that cannabis mocktails should be consumed as carefully as their liquored-up cousins. Have one per hour at most, and don't pick up those car keys.**

## INGREDIENTS

- 1 OUNCE (30 ML) FRESHLY SQUEEZED LIME JUICE, STRAINED

- 1/4 OUNCE FRESHLY SQUEEZED ORANGE JUICE, STRAINED

- 1 OUNCE (30 ML) POMEGRANATE JUICE OR CRANBERRY JUICE

- 1/2-1 OUNCE (15-30 ML) MEDICATED RICH SIMPLE SYRUP (SEE PAGE 43), MADE WITH RAW HONEY

- 2 LIME WEDGES

- ICE

Fill a martini glass with ice and top with a little water. Set aside for a few minutes to chill, then discard the ice water.

Combine the juices in a cocktail shaker filled three-quarters full with ice. Shake hard for 10 seconds. Strain into the chilled martini glass. Sweeten to taste with the Medicated Rich Simple Syrup. Squeeze one wedge of lime over the top of the drink, then garnish with the remaining lime wedge. Serve immediately.

# 07

## WARMING BEVERAGES
### *to Chase Away the Chill*

Some folks detest wintertime, but I have to admit that I love it. I finally get to build wood fires in the fireplace, slip into the soft sweaters that I'd packed away in cedar for the summer months, and relax with a hot drink or two. And that's the idea behind the medicated drinks in this chapter: they're sure to chase the chills right down to Key West.

There's more than one way to defrost, though. Let's start with rum, which has warming, healing properties that are the stuff of legend. Centuries ago, during the Age of Sail, sailors were allocated a pint (!) of rum per day as part of their rations. That's because the drinking water was—well, less than savory—and because they would have had to battle freezing, wet weather and twenty-hour workdays. These days, rum still has the power to warm you from the inside out, and, luckily, dark rum's flavor profile harmonizes well with lots of different strains of cannabis. Try adding your favorite rum-based tinctures to recipes that call for a cannabis tincture.

Rum and warming spices are great chums, too. In fact, spices like cloves, cinnamon, cardamom, and nutmeg seem to heat you up from within all by themselves—no alcohol or cannabis necessary—which is probably why they turn up so often in traditional holiday baked treats, such as gingerbread and pumpkin pie. But the holiday season is a great excuse to use them in warming cannabis cocktails, so skip the chain-store lattés, and make yourself a Seven Hours of Innocence, a tarted-up, black tea–based cocktail that combines rum, a dash of orange liqueur, a pat of Canna-Butter, and a homemade infusion of whichever baking spices are standing to attention in your spice rack.

Or, if you've got a sweet tooth (and who doesn't, especially around the holidays?) you'll love some of the rich, chocolatey concoctions in this chapter. This here is drinkable comfort food, so try Grasshoppers Whirring, a hot chocolate–based beverage that's named for the elegiac sound that heralds summer's end. Chocolate and spice bring out the best in each other, so I've also added a chili-infused rose simple syrup to Grasshoppers as well. It can't do any harm and may do some good, as the old saying goes, because the capsaicins in chiles act as anti-inflammatories and provide an endorphin rush that can combat pain. And a portion of cannabis-infused bourbon doesn't go astray here, either.

If you prefer more bracing, savory winter warmers, this chapter's got something for you, too. A Pirate's Healer, for instance, is a rambunctious combination of bitter, herbal Italian amaro and a tincture made from Indica-infused rum: then it's heated gently until it's barely steaming. You may have had amaro chilled or at room temperature before, but it's just as good when it's warmed through: it's an ideal nightcap.

And don't feel obliged to wait until winter to try these cocktails: lots of them can be transformed to suit warmer weather. Some of them are actually cool drinks with warming properties, such as the Jet Chamber, which comprises vodka, coconut milk, hot Thai spices, and seltzer. Others can be made iced, like She Has Wisdom and She Knows What To Do, which tops up hot or chilled tea with luscious Sorel liqueur. Whatever your poison, avoid having too much of a good thing, and don't have more than one cocktail per hour. Moderation can only enhance the benefits of these warm, fortifying drinks.

# King's Road Toastini

Hot buttered rum is warming and restorative when it's made the traditional way, but this canna-version of hot buttered rum is really the best way I know to chase away a chill. Make it with your favorite black tea, decaf tea, or plain boiling water, but don't skip the pat of butter: it adds heft and healthy fats to the drink. When you're infusing a dark rum, choose an Indica strain such as Pure Kush. It's got that classically skunky, funky aroma, but that's exactly the right flavor pairing for some Jamaican rums, which are made with a wild yeast called dunder. Dunder and Pure Kush share that funky, earthy quality, so they're a well-matched couple. And know this: when I'm enjoying hot drinks that involve cannabis, the herb's effects can sneak right up on me. Your body might not react in quite the same way, but still—leave your car or bicycle in the driveway, and stay put for the next few hours.

## INGREDIENTS

· 1 TEASPOON NON-MEDICATED BUTTER

· 2 OUNCES (60 ML) CANNABIS-INFUSED DARK RUM

· 6 OUNCES (180 ML) HOT, STRONG BLACK TEA OR BOILING WATER

· 2 OUNCES (60 ML) NON-MEDICATED SIMPLE SYRUP (SEE DIRECTIONS BELOW), OR TO TASTE

To make the simple syrup, combine equal parts sugar and hot water. Stir until dissolved.

Preheat a mug by filling it with boiling water and setting it aside for a couple minutes, then pour out the water. Add the butter and rum to the warm mug, then top with the tea or boiling water. Sweeten to taste with the simple syrup, stir gently, and enjoy.

# Seven Hours of Innocence

**This is one of my all-time favorite belly-healers. The recipe is as old as the yacht my family used to own—although the original certainly did not have the Canna-Butter! But it did contain ginger, and so does the Seven Hours of Innocence—in the form of a simple syrup. (Ginger's ability to ease nausea [i.e. seasickness] is well known) Make your infused rum with Sativa-hybrid Red Dragon: like ginger, it's pungent on the nose, but features layers of exotic spices, and it's got a candied-sugar aroma.**

## INGREDIENTS

- 1 OUNCE (30 ML) CANNABIS-INFUSED DARK RUM

- 1/2 OUNCE (15 ML) ORANGE LIQUEUR

- 1 OUNCE (30 ML) NON-MEDICATED GINGER SIMPLE SYRUP (SEE INSTRUCTIONS BELOW)

- 1 TABLESPOON (WEIGHT WILL VARY) WHOLE CARIBBEAN-INFLUENCED SPICES, SUCH AS CARDAMOM, CLOVE, PIECES OF CINNAMON BARK, AND FRAGMENTS OF WHOLE NUTMEG

- 6 OUNCES (180 ML) HOT BLACK TEA, OR USE YOUR FAVORITE TEA INSTEAD

- 1 TEASPOON CANNA-BUTTER (SEE PAGE 44) OR CANNA-COCONUT OIL (SEE PAGE 41)

To make the ginger simple syrup, add 1 cup (200 g) of sugar to 1 cup (235 ml) of boiling water. Mix well, then add a 1-inch (2.5 cm) piece of gingerroot, peeled and thickly sliced. Let cool, transfer to an airtight container, and store in the fridge overnight. Strain through a fine-mesh strainer, and discard the solids. The syrup is now ready to use.

Place the whole spices in a hemp teabag, seal and set aside.

Preheat a mug by filling it with boiling water and setting it aside for a couple minutes, then pour out the water. Add the dark rum, orange liqueur, and ginger simple syrup, then top with the hot tea. Submerge the teabag of spices in the liquid, and let steep for 2 to 3 minutes. Remove the teabag, and top the drink with the Canna-Butter. Serve immediately.

# A Pirate's Healer

~~~~~~~~~~~~~~~~~~~~~~~~~~~~~~~~~~~~~~~~~~~~~~~~~~~~~~~~~~~~~~~~~~~~

Amaro, which means "bitter" in Italian, is an herbal liqueur that was created as a digestive. I can't think of any better way to finish off a long, multi-course meal. (Plus, it just tastes good: no spoonful of sugar necessary to help your medicine go down.) And it's just as good when it's heated. Add a few drops of your favorite cannabis tincture to a portion of amaro. Try a dark rum that you've infused with Indica strain South Central L.A., which has a sweet, rich aroma and an even sweeter taste. It's a great way to balance amaro's bitter, tangy mouthfeel, and if you ask me, it helps promote good digestion and restful sleep. Then, gently heat the amaro for a few moments over steaming water, and enjoy it as a nightcap.

═══════════════════════════╡ INGREDIENTS ╞═══════════════════════════

· 2 OUNCES (60 ML) OF AMARO, COMBINED WITH NO MORE THAN
  5 ML OF YOUR FAVORITE CANNABIS TINCTURE

..........................................................................

Fill a teacup half full with boiling water. Add the infused amaro to a brandy snifter. Heat the snifter by resting it in the teacup until it's warmed through. Remove the snifter carefully: the glass may be hot. When the base of the snifter is cool enough to handle, serve and sip carefully: just a single serving is all you'll need.

# *Grasshoppers Whirring*

It's next to impossible to say no to a mug of hot chocolate—especially when it's this good. And my own recipe for Best Hot Chocolate is a wonderful vehicle for cannabis-infused whiskey. Make yours with a dreamy little Indica strain called Blackberry. It's as darkly flavored as its namesake berry, with notes of smoke, slow-cooked stone fruits, and diesel fuel, and it works so well with the bittersweetness of dark chocolate. The final touch to Grasshoppers Whirring—the one that really sets hearts aflutter—is a portion of chile-infused rose simple syrup. It adds the necessary sweetness, plus extra notes of spice and smoke, to the hot chocolate. (Look for the simple syrup in specialty shops, or online.)

## INGREDIENTS

### For Best Hot Chocolate

- 6 OUNCES (170 G) OF DARK CHOCOLATE
- 6-8 OUNCES (175 TO 235 ML) HEAVY CREAM

### For Grasshoppers Whirring

- 2 OUNCES (60 ML) CANNABIS-INFUSED BARRELL BOURBON WHISKEY
- 2 OUNCES (60 ML) STORE-BOUGHT CHILE-INFUSED ROSE SIMPLE SYRUP
- 6 OUNCES (180 ML) OF MY BEST HOT CHOCOLATE
- GRATED DARK CHOCOLATE, FOR GARNISH

First, make the Best Hot Chocolate. Melt the dark chocolate in a double boiler. Then, whisk in the heavy cream. No need to add sugar: the rose simple syrup will provide sweetness as well as a smoky flavor. Keep warm, stirring constantly, until you're ready to serve.

Preheat a mug by filling it with boiling water and setting it aside for a couple minutes, then pour out the water. Add the whiskey, rose simple syrup, and top with the Best Hot Chocolate. Shave a little dark chocolate over the top of the drink, and serve immediately.

SERVES 2

# The King of New York

I don't often get sick, but it's good to know that if I do, I've got a bottle of healing Krupnikas nearby. Krupnikas is a herbal liqueur that hails from Lithuania, and, at 140 proof, it's not for the faint of heart. But when you add it to hot tea and lemon juice, it becomes the most powerful winter warmer imaginable: it can even combat the Arctic chill that takes over New York City every year between November and March. Make a cannabis-infused Krupnikas with Northern Lights, an Indica strain with flavors that mimic the fire-driven flavors in the liqueur, plus aromatics of sweet pine sap. Remember, though, that The King of New York is strong stuff, so plan on staying near a couch for a couple of hours.

## INGREDIENTS

· 1 OUNCE (30 ML) CANNABIS-INFUSED KRUPNIKAS

· 1/2 OUNCE (15 ML) FRESHLY SQUEEZED LEMON JUICE, STRAINED

· 4 OUNCES (120 ML) VERY STRONG BLACK TEA, SUCH AS IRISH BREAKFAST TEA

· SUGAR OR RAW HONEY, TO TASTE

Preheat a mug by filling it with boiling water and setting it aside for a couple minutes, then pour out the water. Add the Krupnikas and the lemon juice, and top with the hot tea. Sweeten with sugar or raw honey to taste, and serve immediately.

# A Squadron of Ferocious Dragons

Canna-Butter is such a versatile ingredient. You can add it to hot buttered rum, or to Turkish coffee (check out Beside the Bosphorus on page 54). Heck, you can even spread it on toast. But did you ever think about adding it to homemade hot chocolate? If not, you've got to try A Squadron of Ferocious Dragons. Once your hot chocolate is ready and waiting, you add a little applesauce (seriously) and a dash of sea salt to it—plus a healthy pat of Canna-Butter. Make your Canna-Butter with Indica strain Hindu Kush, if you can: its sandalwood aromas meld so well with the applesauce-spiked hot chocolate. The finishing touches are handmade whipped cream and a drizzle of caramel sauce. (If you're making your own caramel, let me offer you this advice: Keep a bucket of ice water handy in case you get burned by the hot molten sugar. You'll thank me later!)

## INGREDIENTS

· 6 OUNCES (180 ML) BEST HOT CHOCOLATE (SEE PAGE 107)

· 1 OUNCE (28 G) APPLESAUCE (HOMEMADE OR STORE-BOUGHT)

· PINCH SEA SALT

· 1 TABLESPOON (14 G) CANNA-BUTTER (SEE PAGE 44)

· FRESHLY WHIPPED CREAM

· 1/4 OUNCE GOOD-QUALITY CARAMEL SAUCE, FOR GARNISH

Preheat a mug by filling it with boiling water and setting it aside for a couple minutes, then pour out the water. Add the Best Hot Chocolate, applesauce, and the sea salt. Top with the Canna-Butter. Serve hot with a dollop of freshly whipped cream, and drizzle with caramel sauce to finish.

# The Thrill of Victory and the Agony of Defeat

Tea and coffee are absolute necessities in my house, but that doesn't mean all hot drinks have to be a single color (that is, brown). And you don't have to limit them to a single type of spirit, either. Expand your horizons with a Thrill of Victory: it's made with Barr Hill's barrel-aged Tom Cat gin, because I love its signature raw honey flavor. Then, it's dressed up with a dash of absinthe, and a fiercely strong simple syrup that's made with rose and saffron, plus curry bitters. When you're infusing the gin for this drink, think about using an Indica strain such as Blue Power. It's got notes of citrus, fresh soil, and dark stone fruits, and it complements the Eastern flavors of saffron and curry incredibly well.

## INGREDIENTS

· 1¼ OUNCES (45 ML) CANNABIS-INFUSED BARR HILL TOM CAT GIN

· 1/10 OUNCE (3 ML) JADE LIQUEURS' ESPRIT EDOUARD ABSINTHE

· 2 OUNCES (60 ML) SAFFRON-INFUSED ROSE SIMPLE SYRUP

· 4 DROPS CURRY BITTERS FROM THE BITTER END

· 6 OUNCES (180 ML) HOT WATER, OR MORE TO TASTE

Preheat a mug by filling it with boiling water and setting it aside for a couple minutes, then pour out the water. Add the gin and the absinthe, followed by the rose simple syrup, and stir well. Top with the hot water, and dot with the curry bitters. Serve immediately.

# *Jet Chamber*

When I'm chilled to the bone, all I can think about is a spicy Thai meal, which seems to heat me up from the inside out. (Funnily enough, I crave exactly the same thing during the summer.) The aromatic Thai spices, including chile, are what really get me going—and they're just as effective when they're served in a cool drink. Infuse a bottle of vodka—yes, vodka!—with Sativa strain Voodoo. It's got herbs, spices, and chile peppers on the nose, so it's the ideal foil for crisp, clear vodka and rich coconut milk. A sprinkle of chiffonaded Thai basil is the only garnish you'll need (but go ahead and use regular basil if you can't get your hands on the Thai variety). The resultant Jet Chamber is madly, mystically warming.

## INGREDIENTS

- 1 OUNCE (30 ML) CANNABIS-INFUSED VODKA
- 1 OUNCE (30 ML) COCONUT MILK
- 1 HAND-CUT ICE CUBE
- 1 LARGE PINCH HOT THAI-SPICE BLEND
- 1-2 OUNCES (30-60 ML) SELTZER WATER
- FEW LEAVES OF THAI BASIL, CHIFFONADED
- 3 DROPS AROMATIC BITTERS

Add the vodka and coconut milk to a rocks glass, and mix gently. Add a hand-cut ice cube, followed by the pinch of spices. Top with a splash of seltzer, and sprinkle with the chiffonaded basil. Dot with the bitters, and sit tight for a while.

# She Has Wisdom and She Knows What to Do

In general, Europeans are miles ahead of their American cousins when it comes to after-dinner drinks and digestives—think of amaro, anisette, German herbal digestives, and raki—which contain tinctures traditionally made from local wild herbs. Americans don't seem to have taken to *digestifs* in quite the same way. But there's an exception to that rule: a Caribbean-inspired Sorel liqueur. Try the version called, simply, Sorel, made by Jack From Brooklyn (www.jackfrombrooklyn.com), with its warming flavors of clove, cassia, ginger, and hibiscus—then transform it into a cannabis infusion. Think about using Sativa strain Tangerine Haze; with its scents of citrus and spices, it's the best partner imaginable for Sorel's exotic taste. And feel free to serve your tea hot or chilled, depending on the weather.

## INGREDIENTS

· 4 OUNCES (120 ML) BREWED HERBAL TEA, SUCH AS LAVENDER AND MINT

· 1 OUNCE (30 ML) CANNABIS-INFUSED SOREL LIQUEUR

· 2-3 DROPS AROMATIC BITTERS

Fill your favorite tea cup with the hot or chilled herbal tea. Top with the Sorel liqueur, then dot with the bitters. Serve immediately.

# South-Bound Suarez

Some winter days feel endless. You can't imagine ever being any colder than you are right now, and you're sure spring is nothing more than a myth. Then, suddenly, a flash of hope strikes: You've spotted that bottle of dark rum that's been living on top of your fridge since September. Grab it, and make yourself a South-Bound Suarez. Okay, so it's not a hot drink, but it *will* warm you right down to your toes, thanks to the restorative rum, the fragrant nutmeg, and a few drops of your favorite medicated tincture. Use one that you've made with Indica strain Gucci OG, which has the power to turn winter into summer right before your eyes. On the nose, it's got dollops of sweet and soft-over-the-tongue lemon cream soda, and that specific aroma that filters in when you park your car under a pine tree in August. When it's mixed into a concentrated tincture, those pine aromatics and flavors really shine.

## INGREDIENTS

- 1 OUNCE (30 ML) DARK RUM
- 10 ML OR LESS OF YOUR FAVORITE CANNABIS TINCTURE
- FRESHLY SCRAPED NUTMEG
- 4 OUNCES (120 ML) Q TONIC WATER
- LIME WEDGE
- CRUSHED ICE

Fill a Boston shaker three-quarters full with ice. Add the rum and the cannabis tincture, and shake hard. Pour the mixture over plenty of crushed ice into a tiki mug, and scrape a little fresh nutmeg over the top. Finish with the tonic water and a lime wedge.

# *Potato Head Blues*

You know those mornings when getting out of bed is as foreign an idea as wearing a Speedo in January? It's so much warmer under the blankets, so you hit the snooze button a few times—and before you know it, you've overslept. (Again.) Well, think of this drink as a potable fleece blanket. It's a mezcal-spiked cup of joe that's been given physic in the form of medicated agave syrup. If I were you, I'd do my medicating with a cannabis tincture that's been made with a sophisticated Indica strain called White Rhino. Its terpenes mimic the aromas of scorched earth and charred firewood, followed by bursts of saline, wet stones, and glycerin, and they're best buddies with both smoky, lush mezcal and strong coffee.

## INGREDIENTS

- 1 TEASPOON INSTANT ESPRESSO POWDER
- 6 OUNCES (180 ML) HOT WATER, OR TO TASTE

- 1 OUNCE (30 ML) QUALITY MEZCAL
- 1/2 OUNCE (15 ML) AGAVE SYRUP, INFUSED WITH NO MORE THAN 10 ML OF YOUR FAVORITE CANNABIS TINCTURE

Preheat a mug by filling it with boiling water and setting it aside for a couple minutes, then pour out the water. Add the espresso powder, and top with fresh hot water to taste. Add the mezcal to "correct" the coffee, then mix in the medicated agave syrup. Serve immediately.

# Walking Across the Sitting Room,
## I Turned the Television On

Mezcal is tequila's mysterious cousin; it's still mostly undiscovered by mainstream drinkers. It's made from the fermented juice of the heart of the maguey plant, and its taste is, I think, earthier, smokier, and more complex than that of tequila. That's good news for cannabis aficionados, since these flavors make it a great partner for Indica strain LA Confidential. This strain sports aromatics of freshly turned earth, spicy pine, and a pungent quality that reminds me of authentic Jamaican rum.

### INGREDIENTS

- 1/2 APRICOT, GRILLED (SEE INSTRUCTIONS BELOW)
- 1 OUNCE (30 ML) CANNABIS-INFUSED MEZCAL
- 1 OUNCE (30 ML) NON-MEDICATED SIMPLE SYRUP
- 1/2 OUNCE (15 ML) FRESHLY SQUEEZED LIME JUICE
- SPLASH OF SELTZER
- 3 DROPS MEXICAN MOLE BITTERS FROM THE BITTER END
- HAND-CUT ICE CUBES

To grill the apricot: Slice it in half and grill on a cast-iron pan or over charcoal for 3 to 4 minutes per side until the apricot is charred. Use half the apricot in this drink, and reserve the other half for a future use.

Using a muddler or the end of a wooden spoon, muddle the grilled apricot in a Boston shaker until mashed. Add the mezcal, simple syrup, and lime juice, and muddle again. Fill the shaker half full with ice. Shake for 15 seconds, then pour into a double Old-Fashioned glass over a hand-cut ice cube. Top with the seltzer, and dot with the Mexican bitters.

CHAPTER

# 08

## COOLING BEVERAGES
### *to Soothe the Brow*

What do you do when the mercury soars and the stickies kick in? For lots of us, desperation strikes. Sweat beads beneath your glasses and trickles down your nose, and something between a sunshower and a rainstorm happens under your (formerly crisply starched) white button-down shirt. It's enough to drive anyone to drink.

If you've got the kind of burning thirst that only the three H's—hazy, hot, and humid—produce, you'll want to check out the cooling, restorative potables in this chapter. They take their inspiration from a number of different cultures around the world, because each culture responds to hot weather in a unique way. In India, for instance, the temperature is usually well north of anything comfortable and manageable (at least, for nonlocals like me), but there's a solution: lassis, traditional Indian drinks that aren't unlike Western smoothies. They're made from fruit, yogurt, and crushed ice, and you can create endless cannabis-infused variations on that theme. Take, for example, the Rose, Saffron, and Cardamom Lassi on page 124, where a dash of cannabis-infused dark rum enhances the drink's exotic flavors.

Warm-weather refreshers are essential in the Middle East, too, and that's what gets me thinking about the Honey Duke Relaxer on page 126. It's a combination of chilled mint tea plus a pat of homemade Canna-Butter and a dash of cream—plus muddled dates, which are a tip of the hat to the Middle Eastern treat, *majoon*. Majoon is a cannabis-laden confection that's a combination of dates, nuts, butter, spices, and hashish, and it's truly mind-bending. (The Honey Duke Relaxer isn't quite as potent, but it's still important to have just one serving per hour, as with all of the drinks in this book.)

In Vietnam, the best way to stay cool is to grab a glass of salted lemonade, which is far more refreshing than the version Westerners are used to—that overly sweet stuff that comes out of a packet or a can. You won't need air-conditioning when you've got a batch of my cannabis-infused Vietnamese Lemonade on hand. (No need to make your own preserved lemons, either; just grab a jar of them at your local Asian market.)

And, of course, in the United States, we know how to deal with sultry weather, too. If you're looking for a brunch-friendly beverage that won't result in an aching head on Monday morning, try A Bloody Good Remedy. It's akin to a Bloody Caesar—the Canadian take on the Bloody Mary—except it's alcohol-free, and it's doctored up with your favorite cannabis tincture. Or, if you're serving a crowd, you could do worse than present your guests with a punch bowl full of my New Orleans–Fizzy Pharmacy Punch: it's sparkling and lemony, and it's laced with a little cannabis-infused simple syrup. Same goes for the Cucumber, Melon, and Mint Cooler: try making a batch in August, when you'll be able to showcase the bounty of your late-summer garden in a punch that's barely-sweetened by a dose of medicated simple syrup.

The cocktails and mocktails in this chapter may not be able to stop you from complaining about the weather, but they *will* be able to refresh and relax you. Enjoy!

# Hoochie Coochie Man

In India, where temperatures regularly hit three figures, cooling beverages are a must. Enter the *lassi*, a yogurt-based drink that's akin to a smoothie. My favorite version features mango puree—or, in a pinch, mango sorbet or sherbet—paired with thick Greek-style yogurt and a snow shower of crushed coconut water ice. If you're making a Hoochie Coochie Man, you'll want to correct it with a little cannabis-infused light rum. Try infusing your rum with Critical Kush, a mostly-Indica strain. It has deep aromatics of Asian spices, freshly turned soil, and a concentrated pungency that's the right contrast for the sweetness of the mango and the yogurt. And there's enlightenment in each sip. (This strain of Kush is a powerful full-body relaxant, though, so no driving or bicycle riding allowed!) Top off your Hoochie with a couple drops of Creole bitters, which were originally invented as a remedy for dysentery.

## INGREDIENTS

- 4 OUNCES (120 ML) MANGO PUREE
- 4 OUNCES (120 ML) GREEK-STYLE YOGURT
- 1 OUNCE (30 ML) CANNABIS-INFUSED LIGHT RUM
- 1 CUP CRUSHED COCONUT WATER ICE
- CREOLE-STYLE BITTERS

Combine all the ingredients in blender and process until smooth. Divide between two Burgundy wine glasses with plenty of freshly crushed coconut water ice. Dot each with a couple drops of the Creole bitters.

SERVES 2

# Rose, Saffron, and Cardamom Lassi

I'm a bit of a lassi addict regardless of the weather, but in summertime, the cravings really kick in. That's why I couldn't resist including a second lassi recipe here—one that's dripping with Asian perfumes of rose, bright-yellow saffron, and green-citrusy cardamom. Cardamom, by the way, is the flavor equivalent of a knife: it slices right through the rich milk fat in the yogurt and milk. This lassi is sweetened with a Medicated Rich Simple Syrup that's been made with raw honey: make yours with Sativa strain Early Pearl. Its aromatics of chocolate, warm spices, and slow-cooked stone fruits add nuance to the lassi's exotic floral flavors. This recipe makes two servings, and it contains plenty of medicated syrup, so don't drink the whole batch yourself—at least not at one sitting.

## INGREDIENTS

- 2 CUPS (460 G) GREEK-STYLE YOGURT
- 3/4 CUP (175 ML) WHOLE MILK
- 4-5 THREADS DRIED SAFFRON, RECONSTITUTED IN 2 TABLESPOONS WARMED MILK, THEN COOLED
- SCANT PINCH OF TURMERIC

- SEEDS FROM 6 CARDAMOM PODS, LIGHTLY CRUSHED
- 1 TABLESPOON (15 ML) ROSEWATER
- 1/4 CUP (60 ML) MEDICATED RICH SIMPLE SYRUP (SEE PAGE 43), MADE WITH RAW HONEY

Place all the ingredients except the Medicated Rich Simple Syrup in a blender and process until smooth and creamy. Add the Medicated Rich Simple Syrup: taste, and add more sugar and rosewater, if required. Blend again. Divide between two Burgundy wine glasses, and top each with a pinch of saffron, if desired.

SERVES 2

# Honey Duke Relaxer

The "bubbles" in bubble tea aren't bubbles at all, of course; they're chewy tapioca pearls. They go so well with a chilled, cream-spiked mint tea—even one that's been muddled with dates and pistachios in a nod to *majoon*, the mind-expanding Moroccan candy made from dates and hashish. When you're making your Honey Duke Relaxer, use a Canna-Coconut Oil that you've infused with Sativa strain Lemon Haze, with its ample aromatics of freshly crushed lemons and Eastern spices like anise, cinnamon, spearmint, and coriander. It's the perfect repartee to the sweetness of the dates and the simple syrup.

## INGREDIENTS

- 1 OUNCE (30 ML) CANNA-COCONUT OIL (SEE PAGE 41)
- 2-3 GRILLED DATES, FOR GARNISH
- SPRINKLE OF FINELY-CRUSHED PISTACHIOS
- 1 OUNCE (30 ML) NON-MEDICATED RAW HONEY SIMPLE SYRUP (SEE PAGE 43)

- 6 OUNCES (180 ML) PEPPERMINT TEA, BREWED, THEN COOLED
- 2 OUNCES (60 ML) DARK RHUM AGRICOLE
- DASH OF HEAVY CREAM
- 1-2 TABLESPOONS COOKED TAPIOCA PEARLS

Fill a Collins glass with ice. Heat the Canna-Coconut Oil for about 15 seconds in the top of a double boiler, until it turns clear. Then remove it from the heat, and add it to the glass.

Muddle the grilled dates with the crushed pistachios in a Boston shaker, then fill the shaker three-quarters full with ice. Add the Raw Honey Simple Syrup, the peppermint tea, the Rhum Agricole, and the heavy cream. Cap and shake hard for 10 seconds.

Place the tapioca pearls on top of the Canna-Coconut Oil in the ice-filled Collins glass. Strain the liquid mixture on top, then serve with a colorful straw.

# Bertha Lee's Baby

After you've gone to all the trouble of preparing a good meal, the last thing you want to do is mess it up by serving a fancy, overly-complicated drink at its end. So don't do it. Instead, serve each of your guests the small, but perfectly formed, Bertha Lee's Baby. It only has three ingredients: grilled orange slices, cannabis-infused mezcal, and cold black coffee. (Well, three-and-a-half, if you count the optional honey.) And it's the ideal after-dinner tipple when the weather's warm. Infuse your mezcal with the soothing Indica-Sativa hybrid strain Colorado Chem. It's sweetly-skunky and lemony, so it plays off both the muddled citrus—its terpenes mimic the flavors of the cannabis—and the bitter, chilled coffee.

## INGREDIENTS

- 3 GRILLED ORANGE SLICES
- 1 OUNCE (30 ML) CANNABIS-INFUSED MEZCAL
- 3 OUNCES (90 ML) COLD, STRONG COFFEE
- RAW HONEY TO TASTE, IF DESIRED

To grill orange slices: Peel and thickly slice 1 orange. Place 3 slices on a hot cast-iron pan (or over charcoal) for 3 minutes per side to help the fruit caramelize. Let cool.

Muddle the cooled, grilled orange slices in a cocktail shaker. Add a handful of ice, then the mezcal, followed by the coffee. Shake hard for 10 seconds. Adjust the sweetness to taste with a little raw honey. Strain into a Collins glass, and serve.

# Lucky Lemon–Mint Iced Earl Grey Tea

**Quit making iced tea with that canned, presweetened powdered junk. Instead, drink this: a cannabis-laced iced Earl Grey tea that's brimming with the refreshing flavors of lemon and mint. In it, sultry Earl Grey meets mystical, smoky Lapsang souchong, and they spend the night together—but they're not alone. Fresh lemon juice and a honey-laden Medicated Rich Simple Syrup keep them company, and the result is both elegant and restorative. Infuse your simple syrup with an Indica strain such as Skywalker. It tastes like candied orange zest and dark blue fruits, which underline the citrusy nature of Earl Grey, and its aroma reminds me of caramelized root vegetables. (That's not as odd as it sounds.) Serve this mocktail to friends at your next picnic lunch.**

## ═══════════╡ INGREDIENTS ╞═══════════

- 2 TEABAGS EARL GREY TEA

- 1 TEABAG LAPSANG SOUCHONG TEA

- 24 OUNCES (700 ML) BOILING WATER

- 1/4 CUP (60 ML) FRESHLY SQUEEZED LEMON JUICE, STRAINED

- 1/4 CUP (60 ML) MEDICATED RICH SIMPLE SYRUP (SEE PAGE 43), MADE WITH RAW HONEY

- CRUSHED ICE

- HANDFUL OF FRESH MINT LEAVES

Place the tea bags in a teapot, and cover with the boiling water. Let steep for 5 to 10 minutes, to taste, then remove and discard the tea bags. Add the lemon juice and the Medicated Rich Simple Syrup, and stir to combine. Let cool and refrigerate overnight.

Fill four Collins glasses with crushed ice. Top each with the chilled iced tea. Garnish each with a few torn mint leaves and serve.

SERVES 4

# Nước Mía
## (Iced, Medicated Vietnamese Sugarcane Juice)

Even if you're not drinking it yourself, there's something inherently refreshing about watching Vietnamese street vendors crush freshly cut sugarcane into brimming glasses of the aromatic juice known as *nước mía*. The juice's sultry flavor is strangely reminiscent of Rhum Agricole from Martinique—and even of Brazil's potent patron spirit, cachaça—just minus the alcohol. Now you can make a medicated version at home. Just top up sugarcane juice with a dose of your THC-Infused Condensed Milk: it'll invigorate you right down to your toes. Make your condensed milk with a Sativa strain, which promotes mental clarity and focus, such as Asian Fantasy. Its spice- and grape-tinged aromatics complement both the sugarcane juice and the rich, sweet milk.

### INGREDIENTS

- COCONUT WATER ICE CUBES
- 6 OUNCES (180 ML) NƯỚC MÍA (FRESH SUGARCANE JUICE), CHILLED
- 2 OUNCES (60 ML) THC-INFUSED CONDENSED MILK (SEE PAGE 40)
- THAI BASIL LEAVES, FOR GARNISH

Fill a Collins glass with coconut water ice cubes. Add the sugarcane juice, and top with the THC-Infused Condensed Milk. Mix gently. Garnish with a leaf or two of Thai basil. Add a colorful straw, and serve immediately.

# French Herb–Scented Vichy Water

If you combine sugar *and* alcohol, the result is, far too often, a knee-knocking hangover. So make yourself a French Herb-Scented Vichy Water instead: it's both booze-free and mercifully low in sugar. First, you'll make a concentrated, tangy, medicated simple syrup. Then, you'll add it to a refreshing pour of sparkling water, before dotting the finished drink with cucumber bitters. Use a Medicated Rich Simple Syrup you've infused with Blue Dream, which boasts a spicy, herbal fragrance and flavors of sugar-coated dark berries and exotic spices.

## INGREDIENTS

### For the herbed simple syrup:

- 2 TABLESPOONS (8 G) DRIED *HERBES DE PROVENCE*
- 1/2 OUNCE (15 ML) MEDICATED RICH SIMPLE SYRUP (SEE PAGE 43), MADE WITH RAW HONEY
- 1 TABLESPOON (15 ML) APPLE CIDER VINEGAR

### For the cocktail:

- LEMON ZEST ICE
- 6 OUNCES (180 ML) VICHY WATER (OR 6 OUNCES PLAIN SELTZER TOPPED WITH A PINCH OF SEA SALT)
- CUCUMBER BITTERS
- LEMON ZEST TWIST

First, make the herbed simple syrup. Place the *herbes de Provence* in a hemp tea bag, and seal. Combine the Medicated Rich Simple Syrup and the apple cider vinegar in a heat-proof mason jar, and immerse the teabag in the liquid. Do not seal the jar. Place the jar in the top of a double boiler. Fill the top of the double boiler with enough water to cover the mason jar halfway. Simmer lightly at no more than 160°F (71°C) for 1 hour. (Use a digital thermometer to keep an eye on the temperature.) Remove the teabag from the syrup mixture, and let cool.

Then, add the lemon zest ice to a Collins glass. Top with 1 ounce (30 ml) of the herbed simple syrup. Top with the Vichy water. Dot with the cucumber bitters, and garnish with a lemon zest twist. Serve immediately.

# A Bloody Good Remedy

Have you ever had a Bloody Caesar? It's the Canadian take on the classic American brunchtime eye-opener, the Bloody Mary, and it contains one unusual ingredient: clam broth. (If you've ever had Manhattan clam chowder, you get the idea.) And it's startlingly delicious. The best part of A Bloody Good Remedy, though, is that it's alcohol-free, so you won't have to deal with a banging head on Monday morning. It's lightly medicated, too: you simply prepare your tomato-clam mixer, toss it over ice, and then add a few drops of your favorite cannabis tincture. Try one that you've infused with Blue OG. Its blue-fruit notes and crushed-woodchip scent are a lovely, if unexpected, partnership with the saline flavors of the clam broth and the spicy tomato base. Oh, and go nuts when it comes to garnishes; the weirder and wackier, the better.

## INGREDIENTS

- 6 OUNCES (180 ML) STORE-BOUGHT TOMATO-CLAM MIXER, CHILLED (OR, YOUR FAVORITE BLOODY MARY MIX COMBINED WITH 1 OUNCE CLAM BROTH)
- NO MORE THAN 2 TEASPOONS (10 ML) OF YOUR FAVORITE CANNABIS TINCTURE
- ASSORTED GARNISHES, SUCH AS OLIVES, CHERRY TOMATOES, CELERY STICKS, LEMON WEDGES, FRESH CHILES, AN ENTIRE SMOKED HERRING, OR EVEN FRIED CHICKEN PIECES

Fill a glass with ice. Add the mixer, followed by the tincture, and stir gently to combine. Strain mixture into glasses. Garnish as much and as creatively as you like!

# Dr. Bamford's Mystery Mocktail

I fell in love with shrubs of all sorts when I was writing *Bitters and Shrub Syrup Cocktails*. So I'm always looking for ways to work the Quick Strawberry-Balsamic Canna-Shrub on page 45 into my cocktails and mocktails, and Dr. Bamford's Mystery Mocktail is one of my favorites. It's simple to make, but it's sophisticated and refreshing, too, so it's an ideal warm-weather aperitif. Make yours with good-quality fruit that's just gone soft: that'll produce the greatest intensity of flavor. Infuse your shrub with Sativa strain Exodus, with its stimulating aromatics of a root cellar post-harvest, followed by fermenting milk. These spicy, earthy qualities work beautifully as a counterpoint to the sweet, tangy notes inherent to white balsamic vinegar.

═══════════════╡ INGREDIENTS ╞═══════════════

· GRAPEFRUIT ZEST TWIST

· CUBE HAND-CUT ICE

· 1 OUNCE (30 ML) QUICK STRAWBERRY-BALSAMIC CANNA-SHRUB (SEE PAGE 45)

· 4 OUNCES (120 ML) SELTZER WATER

· 6 DROPS MÁS MOLE BITTERS FROM AZ BITTERS LAB

· SPRIG OF FRESH MINT, FOR GARNISH

Rub the grapefruit zest around the inside of a rocks glass to release its oils. Then, place the grapefruit twist in the glass. Add one cube of hand-cut ice, and top with the shrub. Add the seltzer water, and finish with exactly six drops of the bitters. Garnish with fresh mint, and serve.

# Vietnamese Lemonade

Simultaneously salty and sweet, Vietnamese lemonade is so much greater than the sum of its parts. And its parts are pretty darn great. For my easy-to-make version, you'll start off with a wedge of Vietnamese preserved lemon. It's not hard to make your own preserved lemons, but they're also available in Asian supermarkets. Then, you'll correct it with a cannabis-infused simple syrup before topping it to taste with bubbling seltzer water. Make your Medicated Rich Simple Syrup with hybrid strain Inferno OG. It picks up the citrus aromatics of the juice, and adds hints of Vietnamese coriander, cinnamon, chile pepper, and baby skunk. You'll have to sit on your hands to keep from pouring yourself a second glass.

 INGREDIENTS

- 1 WEDGE VIETNAMESE PRESERVED LEMON (ABOUT 1/4 LEMON)
- 1 TABLESPOON (15 ML) MEDICATED RICH SIMPLE SYRUP (SEE PAGE 43), MADE WITH RAW HONEY, OR TO TASTE
- 2 OUNCES (60 ML) SELTZER WATER

Using a muddler or the end of a wooden spoon, muddle the preserved lemon wedge in a 6-ounce (180 ml) juice glass. Top with the Medicated Rich Simple Syrup, and cover with the seltzer water. Check for sweetness, and add more simple syrup if necessary. Serve immediately.

# *New Orleans–Style Fizzy Pharmacy Punch*

**Inspired by Louis J. Dufilho, America's first licensed pharmacist, this Pharmacy Punch is best served mid-afternoon, when the sun is at its strongest and when spirits (and appetites) begin to droop. It's powerfully relaxing and terribly refreshing, and I can imagine Mr. Dufilho serving bowls of this bitter-laden punch to his regular customers. He might have made it with salty, mineral-rich, French Vichy water, dispensed from his elaborately hand-carved wooden soda fountain. He may even have used cannabis preparations in it, too, since cannabis was well known to early apothecaries. Make this punch with a Medicated Rich Simple Syrup you've infused with Indica strain Green Dragon. Its aromatics of citrus and spice are natural partners for lemonade.**

## INGREDIENTS

- 1 QUART (950 ML) VIETNAMESE LEMONADE (SEE PAGE 138)

- 1 QUART (950 ML) PLAIN LEMONADE

- 1 CUP (235 ML) MEDICATED RICH SIMPLE SYRUP (SEE PAGE 43), OR TO TASTE

- 1 BOTTLE (750 ML) OF VICHY WATER, OR THE EQUIVALENT AMOUNT OF SELTZER WATER PLUS A PINCH OF SALT

- 10 DASHES EACH OF CREOLE-STYLE BITTERS AND AROMATIC BITTERS

- COCONUT WATER ICE CUBES

- FRESH MINT LEAVES AND LEMON PINWHEELS, FOR GARNISH

Combine the lemonades in a large punch bowl. Add the Medicated Rich Simple Syrup and check for sweetness, adding more simple syrup if required. Add the Vichy water, stir, and then top with the bitters.

To serve, add a coconut water ice cube to a tea cup and pour the punch over the top. Don't add ice directly to the punch; the punch will become too diluted. Garnish each cup with fresh mint and a lemon pinwheel.

SERVES 10

# Cucumber, Melon, and Mint Cooler

Sip by gentle sip, this cool punch is a marvelous way to rehydrate just about any time of day. I like to pour myself a glass after a workout. Because it's infused with a raw honey-based Medicated Rich Simple Syrup, it's lightly-sweet, and it's jammed with summery melon, fresh mint, and European cucumbers. (European or English cucumbers are those long, funky ones that often come wrapped in plastic. They work best here because they don't need to be peeled before use.) Make your infused simple syrup with Sativa strain Cookie Butter. Its rich fragrance of hazelnut butter and butterscotch cookies works so well with the gossamer sweetness of the melon. And watch out: this punch is deceptively easy to drink, so don't overdo it. Wait at least an hour between doses.

## INGREDIENTS

· 1 SMALL, FRAGRANT MELON SUCH AS A MUSKMELON, SEEDED, PEELED, AND SLICED LENGTHWISE INTO 1/2-INCH CRESCENTS

· 2 EUROPEAN CUCUMBERS, SKIN ON

· 2-3 BUNCHES FRESH MINT

· 1/2 CUP (120 ML) MEDICATED RICH SIMPLE SYRUP (SEE PAGE 43), MADE WITH RAW HONEY

· 4 CUPS (950 ML) COOL SPRING WATER

· 1 LARGE BLOCK OF ICE

Add the sliced melon to a punch bowl. Score the cucumbers with a knife lengthwise from top to bottom to release the essential oils in the skin, but do not peel. Then, cut the cucumber into long strips using a knife or a peeler. Add the cucumber strips to the sliced melon in the punch bowl. Slap the mint between your hands to release its oils. Add it to the vessel along with the Medicated Rich Simple Syrup, and stir. Top with the spring water, and add a large block of ice. Stir well again, and transfer to the refrigerator for 2 to 3 hours to combine. (The ice will melt; that's okay.) Serve in coupe glasses.

SERVES 5

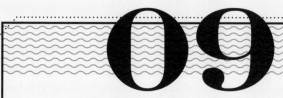

CHAPTER

# 09

## AFTER-DINNER DRINKS:
### *Cannabis Digestives and Nightcaps*

A long, slow-paced meal—the kind that elapses over hours, with multiple courses and wine pairings—is one of life's great pleasures. And you usually end up feeling pretty happily stuffed afterwards. That's when I head for the couch, put my feet up (shoes off, of course), and enjoy a snifter of something that says "dessert."

And "dessert" is open to interpretation. It doesn't have to be filling or heavy. In fact, it doesn't even have to be sweet. Sometimes, it can mean a simple digestive liqueur, like a glass of amaro or anisette. Or it can mean a little bit of rum, brandy, cognac, or whiskey—and then there's the litany of flavored schnapps, cordials, dessert wines, eaux de vies, and aged tequilas as well. All of these spirits have the same goal: to facilitate proper digestion at a meal's end, and to help you ease yourself into a good night's sleep.

S ome cannabis strains can promote relaxation and restfulness as well, especially Indica strains, which are known for their sedative effects. That's why many of the drinks in this chapter include spirits that have been treated to an Indica infusion, while others get their medicine in the form of an Indica-rich pat of homemade Canna-Butter or Canna-Oil. Some of them feature strong coffee—a time-honored way to bring a festive dinner to a happy conclusion. If you can't imagine an evening meal without a coffee chaser, try a No One Makes Me Close My Eyes on page 143. It combines black coffee with a dash of cream and a portion of cannabis-infused rum, finished with a scraping of nutmeg. (Nutmeg itself has been used by traditional healers to relieve pain and ease digestive disorders.) Or, if you'd rather finish your meal with a short, cool drink, try And Everything Is Green and Submarine on page 142, where a coffee liqueur takes the place of *caffè*: it's mixed with a little homemade hot chocolate and a medicated condensed milk before it's shaken with ice, then strained and served with a dot or two of orange bitters.

Then again, you might be in the habit of reaching for a cup of tea when dinner's done. If so, try treating yourself and a friend to a round of Your Mind and Your Inner Dreams on page 146, which combines chilled tea, fresh lemon juice, and cannabis-infused

bourbon in a short slurp that's balanced between tangy and sweet. Or you can skip the caffeinated tea and coffee altogether, and make a batch of my Medicated Apple Ice Wine. (After all, an apple a day keeps the doctor away, right?) Apple ice wine is wonderful on its own, but it's even better when you infuse it with an Indica strain for a full-body chill-out.

And I beg you to try an Ardent Dreamer, a bracing, citrusy, palate-cleansing cocktail that starts with a slice of grilled grapefruit. (I know, grilling does involve a little prep work, but try not to skip this step: it's worth it.) Then it gets dosed with a Sativa-infused tequila, and a little orange liqueur—and before you know it, you'll be nodding off at the table.

At the end of the day, the purpose of good digestives and nightcaps is to bring you and your guests together for one last time before you head off in search of your feather beds and fluffy down comforters. So whichever *digestif* you choose, be sure to go slow and savor every last drop; it's the best way to enjoy all of the handcrafted drinks in this book.

# And Everything Is Green and Submarine

You know that fleeting feeling of complete and utter relaxation you experience right before you fall asleep? Wouldn't it be great if it could be bottled and sold? I haven't figured out how to do that yet, but in the meantime, And Everything Is Green and Submarine is a pretty good substitute. It's the ideal way to bring a leisurely meal with friends to a close, because it combines coffee, dessert, and medication in a single glass. (Focus on the word "single": don't drink doubles. Overdoing it is no fun.) I love making the THC-Infused Condensed Milk for this recipe with Indica hybrid strain Training Day; it's tinged with spices, pine resin, and deep blue fruits, and it'll weave its way into your dreams for sure.

## INGREDIENTS

· HAND-CUT ICE CUBE

· 1 OUNCE (30 ML) COFFEE LIQUEUR

· 1 OUNCE (30 ML) THC-INFUSED
CONDENSED MILK (SEE PAGE 40)

· 1 OUNCE (30 ML) COOLED HOT
CHOCOLATE, SUCH AS MY BEST HOT
CHOCOLATE ON PAGE 107

· ORANGE BITTERS

Add a large ice cube to a rocks glass. Pour in the coffee liqueur, then top with the condensed milk. Finish with the cooled hot chocolate, and add a dash or two of orange bitters.

# *No One Makes Me Close My Eyes*

The things I like to drink after a filling meal can be counted on the fingers of one hand, and rum gets the thumb: that is, it's number one on my list. It's a relaxing, meditative drink. As I'm sipping, I often conjure up the ghosts of sailing vessels past, whose hardworking sailors may have finished their repasts with the very same spirit. Here I combine cannabis-infused rum with a little strong coffee, a dash of cream, and a scraping of nutmeg for a simple but satisfying *digestif*. Try infusing your bottle of aged rum with Indica strain Whitaker Blues, which smacks of deep blue fruits, leading to bourbon vanilla, citrus zest, freshly turned soil, and, finally, sea salt–slicked stones in the finish: this sweet-and-spicy strain complements both the rum and the coffee.

## INGREDIENTS

- 1 OUNCE (30 ML) NON-MEDICATED HEAVY CREAM

- 1½ OUNCES (45 ML) CANNABIS-INFUSED AGED RUM

- 4 OUNCES (120 ML) STRONG BLACK COFFEE

- SCRAPING OF FRESH NUTMEG

- SUGAR OR RAW HONEY (OPTIONAL)

Preheat a mug by filling it with boiling water and setting it aside for a couple minutes, then pour out the water.

Add the heavy cream and the rum to the mug, then top with the hot coffee. Scrape a little nutmeg over the top, and sweeten with sugar or raw honey, if desired.

# The Future Is Uncertain and the End Is Always Near

I use Rhum Agricole in all of my rum-based cocktails. It's made from freshly crushed sugarcane—unlike most of the mainstream stuff, which is derived from industrially-produced molasses. And the only thing better than Rhum Agricole is VSOP Rhum Agricole. "VSOP" stands for "Very Special Old Pale," and it designates a rhum that's been aged in barrels made of French white oak. Get your hands on a bottle if you can: then, medicate it with Indica-hybrid Skunk 47, and use it in an after-dinner The Future Is Uncertain. Skunk 47 takes to the toasty flavors of the Rhum and the grilled kiwi fruit so well. Its scent is like a baby skunk—one with a really bad attitude, because it's all over you from the minute you smell it. But that's a good thing, because the baby-skunk scent quickly gives way to notes of black coffee, leading to freshly turned soil, and saddle leather.

## INGREDIENTS

- 1/2 KIWI, GRILLED (SEE DIRECTIONS BELOW)
- 2 OUNCES (60 ML) CANNABIS-INFUSED VSOP RHUM AGRICOLE
- 1/4 OUNCE ORGEAT SYRUP
- 1 LARGE CUBE COCONUT WATER ICE

To grill the kiwi: Peel a kiwi and cut it in half lengthwise. Place the fruit cut side down on a hot cast-iron pan for 2-3 minutes per side to help the fruit caramelize. Let cool.

Using a muddler or the end of a wooden spoon, muddle the grilled kiwi in a Boston shaker. Add 1 ounce of the Rhum Agricole, then continue to muddle. Add the orgeat syrup, and fill the shaker three-quarters full with ice. Add the rest of the Rhum Agricole, then cap and shake hard for 10 seconds. Pour the mixture into a rocks glass over a large cube of coconut water ice, and serve immediately.

# Your Mind and Your Inner Dreams

~~~

**Bourbon-based beverages make a mighty end to a good meal, and Your Mind and Your Inner Dreams certainly falls into that category. In this whiskey-based after-dinner cocktail, bourbon meets fresh lemon juice meets chilled tea—smoky Lapsang souchong and head-clearing yerba maté—in a toddy that's both refreshing and relaxing. Infuse your whiskey with Indica-dominant hybrid Cornbread. It has a pleasantly dank quality that reminds me of a root cellar, and a lemony scent that complements the fresh lemon juice and highlights the sweetness of the raw honey. And it's just the thing to help you wind down before bed. (Stick to one serving, though: overmedicating won't help you sleep.)**

## INGREDIENTS

- 2 OUNCES (60 ML) CANNABIS-INFUSED BARRELL BOURBON WHISKEY

- 1/2 OUNCE (15 ML) FRESHLY SQUEEZED LEMON JUICE

- 4 OUNCES (120 ML) STRONGLY-BREWED LAPSANG SOUCHONG TEA, COOLED

- 1 TEASPOON RAW HONEY, OR TO TASTE

- 1/2 OUNCE (15 ML) BREWED YERBA MATÉ TEA, COOLED

- 4 DASHES AROMATIC BITTERS

- ICE

...................................................................................................

Fill a cocktail mixing glass three-quarters full with ice. Add all the ingredients except the bitters. Stir well, then strain the mixture into 2 coupe glasses. Dot each with the bitters, and serve immediately.

SERVES 2

# Medicated Apple Ice Wine

If you've already fallen for the crisp flavor of grape-based ice wine, you've got to try apple ice wine. It's made the same way as its vinous cousin: frozen apples have an intense flavor that's concentrated by the cold weather, and when they're harvested and crushed, a naturally-occurring yeast begins the fermentation process. The result is an after-dinner treat that'll haunt your gastronomic memory for years to come. Try making a medicated version of it with beguiling Indica strain Reclining Buddha, which complements the ice wine's aromatics and sweet flavors. It's cherry-scented, spicy, and sweet with a background of crushed stones and forest floor. Turn your infused ice wine into a cocktail by topping it with seltzer water and a dash of aromatic bitters.

## INGREDIENTS

4 GRAMS OF DECARBED CANNABIS, SUCH AS INDICA STRAIN RECLINING BUDDHA

1 BOTTLE (375 ML) OF APPLE ICE WINE

Place the decarbed cannabis in a hemp tea bag. Add the apple ice wine to a medium-size, heat-proof mason jar (the jar should be about half full). Add the cannabis tea bag to the jar. Leave the jar uncovered, and place it in a double boiler on a hot plate or electric stove top. Fill the top of the double boiler with enough water to cover the mason jar halfway. Simmer for 1 hour at no more than 160°F (71°C), using a digital thermometer to keep an eye on the temperature. (Make sure the double boiler doesn't run out of hot water.) Remember to keep your workspace well ventilated.

Some of the liquid will evaporate: when this occurs, add fresh apple ice wine to bring it back up to the desired volume, and stir well.

Remove the ice wine from the heat and let cool. Remove and discard the tea bag. Chill the jar by placing it in a bowl of ice water. Strain the ice wine through a fine-mesh sieve lined with cheesecloth, then funnel back into the bottle. Serve in 3-ounce (90 ml) portions in dessert wine glasses.

# I Danced with the Pearl of Rainy Weather

**Mezcal is tequila's more spiritual sister. She has great mystical powers, and you should never underestimate her powerful healing properties. Infuse your mezcal with cannabis, and you've got a potent healing potion indeed. Use it in I Danced with the Pearl of Rainy Weather, which is, I think, my favorite cocktail in this book. In it, mezcal is combined with black coffee and a chile-infused rose simple syrup that adds mystery to every sip. Then, it's topped with palate-lifting seltzer water and a dash of belly-friendly bitters. When you're making your infusion, try Indica hybrid strain Ancient Kush, which is packed with flavors of lemon and earth: it's a great match for a smoky, single-village mezcal, and it's incredibly soothing and relaxing.**

## INGREDIENTS

- 1½ OUNCES (45 ML) CANNABIS-INFUSED MEZCAL (OPT FOR A SMOKY, SINGLE-VILLAGE VERSION)

- 4 OUNCES (120 ML) STRONG BLACK COFFEE, CHILLED

- 1 OUNCE (30 ML) THREE CHILE SIMPLE SYRUP FROM ROYAL ROSE

- 2 OUNCES (60 ML) SELTZER WATER

- SEVERAL DROPS MÁS MOLE BITTERS FROM AZ BITTERS LAB

Combine the mezcal, coffee, and simple syrup in a mixing glass filled three-quarters full with ice. Strain into two couple glasses. Splash each with the seltzer, and dot with the bitters. Serve one to a friend—and remember to wait at least an hour before making a second round.

# Ardent Dreamer

Orange-cognac liqueur is a fine way to bring a meal to its conclusion (and it makes a great nightcap, too), but you don't necessarily have to take it neat. Pair with the best *añejo* tequila you can find, and use it to make yourself an Ardent Dreamer. You'll want to grill a couple grapefruit slices before adding them to the mix so they're charred and caramelized—all the better to enhance the flavor of the aged tequila. Speaking of which, try medicating your tequila by infusing it with Sativa-dominant hybrid Gatekeeper OG. It's redolent of pine and freshly turned soil, aromatics that seem to melt into the grapefruit's toasted sweetness. A blissful night's rest lies in your future, for sure.

## INGREDIENTS

- 1 THICK SLICE PINK GRAPEFRUIT, GRILLED AND COOLED (SEE DIRECTIONS BELOW)
- 1 OUNCE (30 ML) CANNABIS-INFUSED EXTRA-*AÑEJO* TEQUILA
- 1/2 OUNCE (15 ML) ORANGE-COGNAC LIQUEUR
- ORANGE ZEST TWIST
- 1 GLÄCE LUXURY ICE MARIKO SPHERE

To grill the grapefruit: Slice the ends off the grapefruit and cut it into 1/2-inch rounds. Place the grapefruit slices on a hot cast-iron pan for 2 to 3 minutes per side to help the fruit caramelize. Let cool.

Using a muddler or the end of a wooden spoon, muddle the grilled grapefruit slice in a cocktail mixing glass to release its juices and essential oils. Fill the glass three-quarters full with ice, then add the infused tequila and the orange-cognac liqueur. Cap and shake hard. Pour over a single Gläce Luxury Ice Mariko Sphere in a rocks glass, and garnish with the orange zest twist.

# Monterey Is a Special Place

I love to finish dinner with a portion of neat VSOP Rhum Agricole or an espresso—or even both. But when you're not in the mood for post-prandial coffee or neat spirits (and that does happen from time to time), mix yourself a Monterey Is a Special Place. This fruity, effervescent, after-dinner cocktail is best made with a Scotch whiskey you've infused with a relaxing Indica strain, like Grandaddy Purple (also known as Grandaddy Purp, or GDP). It smacks of fresh blue fruits, charred marshmallows, and baby skunks trapped in a pillowcase under your bed. You'll be surprised at how well its flavors work with smooth blended Scotch. It's a great way to prepare yourself for sleep, too: it'll be lights-out before long.

## INGREDIENTS

- 2 OUNCES (60 ML) FRUITATIONS CRANBERRY MIXER

- 1 OUNCE (30 ML) CANNABIS-INFUSED BLENDED SCOTCH WHISKEY

- 1/2 OUNCE (15 ML) FRESHLY SQUEEZED LEMON JUICE

- 2 OUNCES (60 ML) SELTZER WATER

- GREENISH COCKTAIL CHERRY (SEE PAGE 45), FOR GARNISH

- HAND-CUT ICE CUBES

Fill a cocktail mixing glass three-quarters full with ice. Add the Fruitations mixer, then the Scotch and the lemon juice. Stir 40 times, no more and no less (don't ask questions, just do it). Strain over hand-cut ice cubes into two rocks glasses, then top each with the seltzer. Garnish with a Greenish Cocktail Cherry, and serve immediately.

SERVES 2

# Non-Alcoholic Chamomile Tea Tonic

**Back in the early days of the apothecary, the pharmacist might have been asked to prepare tonics to treat sleep disorders—and one way to do that is to make a tonic from a chamomile tea infusion. And, after the liquid has reduced considerably, you can also add a pat of Canna-Coconut Oil to it for extra medication. An Indica strain like Afghani will help you welcome the Sandman with open arms. Even its aromatics are calming and warming; they're reminiscent of Indian patchouli, sandalwood, warm soil, and citrus zest. Use this Chamomile Tea Tonic with seltzer or in craft cocktails—or take a tablespoon neat about an hour before bed. Sweet dreams!**

## INGREDIENTS

- 2 CUPS (475 ML) WATER
- 2 TABLESPOONS (2-3 G) DRIED CHAMOMILE
- 2 TEASPOONS (7 G) RAW HONEY, OR TO TASTE
- 1 TEASPOON CANNA-COCONUT OIL (SEE PAGE 41)

Place the chamomile in a mesh tea ball. Heat the water in a medium saucepan until it's steaming-hot, but not boiling. Add the tea ball to the hot water, and simmer at no more than 175°F (79°C) for 20 to 30 minutes. Remove the tea ball, and transfer the mixture to a fresh saucepan. Continue to simmer until the mixture has reduced by at least half, or even by three-quarters. Sweeten to taste with the raw honey, and stir in the Canna-Coconut Oil. Mix well to combine. Store in the refrigerator for up to 1 month.

# Spirits, Bar Equipment, and Other Supplies

AZ Bitters Lab
*azbitterslab.com*

Caledonia Spirits
(Barr Hill gin)
*caledoniaspirits.com*

Barrell Bourbon
*barrellbourbon.com*

The Bitter End
*bitterendbitters.com*

Boston Shaker
*thebostonshaker.com*

Jersey Artisan Distilling
(Busted Barrel rum)
*jerseyartisandistilling.com*

Fruitations (craft soda &
cocktail mixers)
*justaddfruitations.com*

Jade Liqueurs (absinthe)
*bestabsinthe.com*

Magical Butter Machine
*magicalbutter.com*

Q Drinks (Q Tonic)
*qdrinks.com*

Art in the Age
(root tea liqueur)
*artintheage.com*

Royal Rose Syrups
*royalrosesyrups.com*

Jack From Brooklyn
(Sorel liqueur)
*jackfrombrooklyn.com*

Uncouth Vermouth
*uncouthvermouth.com*

# References & Resources

Deiana, Serena. "Medical use of cannabis. Cannabidiol: a new light for schizophrenia?." *Drug testing and analysis* 5, no. 1 (2013): 46-51.

Feliú, A., M. Moreno-Martet, M. Mecha, F. J. Carrillo-Salinas, E. Lago, J. Fernández-Ruiz, and C. Guaza. "A Sativex (®)-like combination of phytocannabinoids as a disease-modifying therapy in a viral model of multiple sclerosis." *British journal of pharmacology* 172, no. 14 (2015): 3579-3595.

Iuvone, Teresa, Giuseppe Esposito, Daniele De Filippis, Caterina Scuderi, and Luca Steardo. "Cannabidiol: a promising drug for neurodegenerative disorders?." *CNS neuroscience & therapeutics* 15, no. 1 (2009): 65-75.

Lynch, Mary E., and Fiona Campbell. "Cannabinoids for treatment of chronic non-cancer pain; a systematic review of randomized trials." *British journal of clinical pharmacology* 72, no. 5 (2011): 735-744.

Russo, Ethan B. "Taming THC: potential cannabis synergy and phytocannabinoi-terpenoid entourage effects." *British journal of pharmacology* 163, no. 7 (2011): 1344-1364.

Schubart, C. D., I. E. C. Sommer, P. Fusar-Poli, L. de Witte, R. S. Kahn, and M. P. M. Boks. "Cannabidiol as a potential treatment for psychosis." *European Neuropsychopharmacology* 24, no. 1 (2014): 51-64.

Beyond Chronic: Medical Cannabis Information You Can Trust (blog): *http://beyondchronic.com/*

Center for Medicinal Cannabis Research at the University of California, San Diego: *www.cmcr.ucsd.edu/*

Coalition for Cannabis Standards and Ethics: *www.ccsewa.org/*

LeBlanc CNE: Cannabis Genetics, Software, and Biopharmaceuticals: *www.leblanccne.com/*

The National Organization for the Reform of Marijuana Laws: *http://norml.org/marijuana/medical*

# About the Author

**Warren Bobrow** is the creator of the popular blog cocktailwhisperer.com and the author of *Apothecary Cocktails*, *Whiskey Cocktails* and *Bitters & Shrub Syrup Cocktails*.

Warren has taught classes on spirits and cocktails all over the world, including an advanced class on rum at the Moscow Bar Show. He's taught the fine art of social media and food writing at the New School in New York as well as classes on creative cocktails and mocktails at Stonewall Kitchen in Maine.

Warren has written hundreds of articles on cocktails and food for *Chilled Magazine, Saveur, Whole Foods/ Dark Rye, Total Food Service, Eater, Voda, Serious Eats, Foodista, Distiller, Sip and Beverage Media* as well as many other international outlets. He has also written for the *Oxford Encyclopedia: Savoring Gotham* issue and the *Sage Encyclopedia of Food Issues*. He has forthcoming research being published in the *Dishing Up New Jersey* by Wiley Publishing.

Warren was a 2010 Ministry of Rum judge and was the only American food journalist asked to participate in Fete de la Gastronomie, a nationwide celebration of French cuisine in Burgundy.

# Index

# Index

CANNABIS COCKTAILS, MOCKTAILS, AND TONICS

# Index

# Index